SACRAMENTO PUBLIC LIBRARY
828 "I" Street
95814

D0129050

Gluten-Free

Made Simple

EASY EVERYDAY MEALS THAT EVERYONE CAN ENJOY

Gluten-Free

Made Simple

CAROL FIELD DAHLSTROM,
ELIZABETH DAHLSTROM BURNLEY, &
MARCIA SCHULTZ DAHLSTROM

St. Martin's Griffin
New York

Gluten-Free Made Simple
Copyright © 2011 by Carol Field
Dahlstrom, Inc. All rights reserved.
Printed in China.

For information, address St. Martin's
Press, 175 Fifth Avenue,
New York, N.Y. 10010.
www.stmartins.com

The written instructions, recipes, and
photographs in this volume are intended
for personal use of the reader and may
be reproduced for that purpose only.

Library of Congress Cataloging-in-
Publication Data Available Upon Request

ISBN: 978-0-312-55066-0

First Edition: June 2011

10 9 8 7 6 5 4 3 2 1

While all the information in this book has
been tested and checked and every attempt
made to be sure that every recipe is accurate
and gluten-free, human error can occur.
Carol Field Dahlstrom Inc., cannot be held
responsible for any loss or injury associated
with the making of any recipe in this book.

Authors:
Carol Field Dahlstrom,
Elizabeth Dahlstrom Burnley,
Marcia Schultz Dahlstrom

Book Design:
Lyne Neymeyer

Photography: Jay Wilde

How-to Photos: Primary Image: Dean Tanner
and Katy Downy

Copy Editing: Spectrum Communication Services, Inc.

Nutritional Analysis: Elizabeth Dahlstrom Burnley, MS;
Crystal Tallman, RD, LD

Proofreading: Janet Figg, Dr. Michael Dahlstrom

Food Stylist: Carol Field Dahlstrom

Props and Location: Roger Dahlstrom

Technical Assistant: Judy Bailey

Recipe Development and Testing: Elizabeth
Dahlstrom Burnley, Carol Field Dahlstrom, Marcia
Schultz Dahlstrom, Ardith Field, Barbara Hoover,
Twylla Sonquist

Prepress: Integrity Printing, Des Moines, Iowa

Visit us at www.gluten-freemadesimple.com or
www.gfmadesimple.com for gluten-free updates,
more recipes, and tips.

The Story of **Gluten-Free Made Simple**

The combination of authors, each coming to the book from a different angle, makes this book unique and well thought out. An experienced and well-known cookbook author (Carol), a nutritionist specializing in gluten-free cooking at a science-based university (Elizabeth), and a busy wife and mother with celiac disease and first-hand experience living gluten-free (Marcia) collaborated to create a gluten-free cookbook that is simple to use, calls for easy-to-find ingredients, and shares tested recipes that are sure to please you and your family.

Three women, all connected by interest and family, began to accumulate and test hands-on recipes for those with celiac disease and those who choose to live a gluten-free lifestyle. It began because of a need, the expertise was nearby, and everyone wanted and needed it to work.

Because of the need for a practical cookbook that Marcia and her family could use every day, Carol, Elizabeth, and Marcia began to develop gluten-free recipes. Some recipes were good, and some not so good. Recipes were adjusted to improve taste, texture, and quality. Marcia gave her honest opinion about every recipe, as did the whole family. Elizabeth provided information about gluten substitutes and Carol and Marcia explored all kinds of possibilities. The whole family decided that gluten-free meals must be inexpensive and delicious and soon gluten-free recipe development became the family pastime. Dozens of delicious recipes that really worked without using odd or expensive ingredients were developed. And so a cookbook began.

No, we don't all eat gluten-free all the time, although Marcia will eat gluten-free forever. Marcia and her husband Michael won't know if their children will need to eat gluten-free until later in their lives. But for now, we have created a cookbook that really works with recipes that we all enjoy—and we are going to share it with you.

Carol Field Dahlstrom,
Elizabeth Dahlstrom Burnley, and
Marcia Schultz Dahlstrom

About the Authors

Carol Field Dahlstrom was Executive Editor at *Better Homes and Gardens®* books for more than 20 years, producing more than 80 books in the crafts, food, and decorating areas. She is now president of her own company, Brave Ink Press™, and has authored 15 books from that company. She has appeared on many media shows including the *NBC Weekend Today Show* sharing her recipes and ideas. She is frequently featured in national lifestyle magazines and industry periodicals and her business web sites resonate with thousands of readers that follow her work and buy her books. She holds a Master's degree in Education and Art and Design.

Elizabeth Dahlstrom Burnley, Carol's daughter, has a Master's degree in Nutritional Science and is a faculty member teaching nutrition classes at Iowa State University. While studying for her degree she developed an interest in the much-misunderstood concept of gluten and gluten-free cooking. In addition to her other nutrition classes, Elizabeth now teaches classes on gluten-free cooking at Iowa State University to students who want to learn more about this nutritional topic. She is often asked for a gluten-free cookbook that is easy to use. Her classes are filling up faster each semester and interest is growing about this recent and important nutritional area.

Marcia Schultz Dahlstrom, Carol's daughter-in-law, has celiac disease—an autoimmune disease triggered by eating gluten. Marcia has a BA degree in Communications and works part time for a magazine. She has followed a gluten-free diet for four years. Marcia and her husband Michael have two young children and a busy lifestyle, and neither are gourmet cooks. They don't want to spend a fortune on gluten-free purchased foods, and they don't have time for complicated recipes. Along with Carol and Elizabeth, Marcia and Michael have been experimenting and developing recipes to fit their very important need to eat as a gluten-free family.

Contents

About the Book

This book is designed to provide easy-to-find ingredients, simple methods, and delicious recipes for people eating a gluten-free diet. You don't have to be a gourmet chef to cook gluten-free. We have adapted many all-time favorite recipes by making only a few minor changes. Other recipes were more difficult to adapt, but we found ways to substitute ingredients or use easy-to-find and inexpensive flours to make the recipes oh-so-tasty.

Cost and Availability
Many gluten-free product mixes, such as cake and cookie mixes, are expensive and hard to find. Some of these mixes are tasty but some are not. But you can make your own gluten-free recipes for a fraction of the cost, and make them again and again.

Common Methods
Preparing gluten-free recipes doesn't mean that you need to expect complicated ingredients or methods. All of the recipes in this book use common cooking methods and simple ingredients

to give extraordinary results. You'll be amazed just how easy and inexpensive it can be to cook gluten-free!

Nutritional Analysis
We know that if you are eating gluten-free, you are concerned about your health and well-being. Some of you may also be concerned about other food allergies or health problems. So in addition to the box containing the Nutrition Per Serving on each page, we are also telling you if the recipe is vegetarian, low fat,

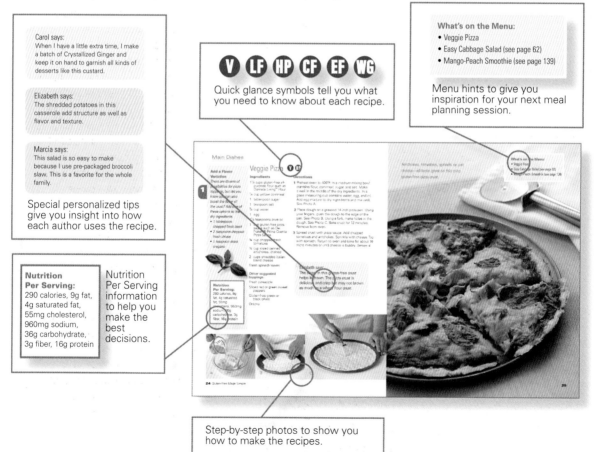

Carol says:
When I have a little extra time, I make a batch of Crystallized Ginger and keep it on hand to garnish all kinds of desserts like this custard.

Elizabeth says:
The shredded potatoes in this casserole add structure as well as flavor and texture.

Marcia says:
This salad is so easy to make because I use pre-packaged broccoli slaw. This is a favorite for the whole family.

Special personalized tips give you insight into how each author uses the recipe.

Nutrition Per Serving:
290 calories, 9g fat, 4g saturated fat, 55mg cholesterol, 960mg sodium, 36g carbohydrate, 3g fiber, 16g protein

Nutrition Per Serving information to help you make the best decisions.

Quick glance symbols tell you what you need to know about each recipe.

What's on the Menu:
• Veggie Pizza
• Easy Cabbage Salad (see page 62)
• Mango-Peach Smoothie (see page 139)

Menu hints to give you inspiration for your next meal planning session.

Step-by-step photos to show you how to make the recipes.

high protein, casein- or dairy-free, egg-free, and if it contains a whole grain. This gives you a better idea of whether the recipe fits into your menu. Beside each of the recipe names we have included an icon that indicates if the recipe is Vegetarian (V) (some recipes contain chicken broth), Low Fat (LF) (less than 8 grams per serving), High Protein (HP) (more than 10 grams per serving), Casein-Free (CF) (free of dairy products), Egg-Free (EF) (free of egg products), and whole grain (WG), if the recipe contains whole grains.

Step-by-Step Photos

Because we want your gluten-free recipe to turn out just right, we often include step-by-step photos to show you how to make the recipe. "A picture is worth a thousand words," and we give you hundreds of photos to assist you. We include these step-by-step photos whenever we think they will help you make the recipe more easily.

Tips and Facts

On each page we give you tips about the recipe featured. Often we give suggestions for freezing or making part of the recipe ahead of time. We even tell you where to find a particular product. Sometimes we tell you how to be certain the purchased ingredients you are using in the recipe are indeed gluten-free, and we give you tips on how to read the labels. Sometimes we give you ideas on flavor variations such as substituting asparagus for snap peas or adding ham to a potato recipe. We even share some special health benefits about certain grains and other foods that might be new to you.

Our Comments

Throughout the book you'll see comments from Carol, Elizabeth, or Marcia about the recipes. Because all of these recipes were developed, tested, and retested over and over again, each of the women learned a lot about the recipes—how they were developed and why, and how they like to enjoy them now. You'll enjoy reading these little quotes throughout the book. All the recipes were developed and tested in kitchens just like yours and the goal was to make them for real people just like you.

About Gluten-Free All-Purpose Flours

You may wonder why we often list the exact flour brand. First, gluten-free all-purpose flours from various companies vary a great deal in their content. Some are primarily made with bean flour, some with tapioca flour or rice flour, and some with a complicated mix of flours. If you choose to substitute a different flour mix than we have suggested, your recipe may not turn out quite the same. It may not even be successful. Second, all of the flours recommended in this book can be ordered online or are easily found in large supermarkets across the country. Third, we want to provide you with the least expensive alternative when making the recipe without giving up flavor, texture, or visual appeal.

Remember that each brand of all-purpose gluten-free flour has its own special characteristics. While various brands of all-purpose wheat-based flours are almost identical, brands of gluten-free all-purpose flours are not.

About Gluten and Celiac Disease

What is gluten?

In the context of gluten-free cooking, gluten refers to specific proteins that are found in wheat, rye, and barley. Therefore, gluten is found in most types of breakfast cereals and breads. It is also added to many other food products for thickening or as a binding ingredient.

In scientific terms, gluten is a protein complex formed from two proteins found only in wheat (glutenin and gliadin). However, when discussing celiac disease, the term "gluten" has come to mean any proteins that cause a celiac response, such as those in wheat, rye, barley, and possibly oats.

What is celiac disease?

Celiac disease is an inherited autoimmune disease that affects the digestive processes of the small intestine. It is also known as gluten sensitive enteropathy, celiac sprue, and nontropical sprue. ("Sprue" refers to a disease of the small intestine.) The prevalence of celiac disease in the United States is estimated as 1 out of 133, which equals more than 3 million Americans. In fact, more people in the U.S. have celiac disease than Alzheimer's disease.

Celiac disease is genetic, and because of the way it is inherited, females have celiac disease more often than males. The disease may begin when the individual is a child, but in other cases the disease is triggered by severe stress, such as after surgery, pregnancy, puberty, childbirth, viral infection, or emotional stress.

When people with celiac disease eat gluten, it creates a reaction that destroys the villi of the small intestine and interferes with food and nutrient absorption. The disease is vastly under-diagnosed because the symptoms of celiac resemble those of many other diseases. Over 300 symptoms have been observed in people with celiac disease, including intestinal problems, abdominal pain, aching joints, skin rashes, anemia, and infertility. It is estimated that only about 5 percent of people with celiac disease have been diagnosed because symptoms are difficult to pinpoint.

Celiac disease is a serious condition, and the only treatment is consuming a 100% gluten-free diet for the person's entire life. If a person with celiac disease continues to eat gluten, his/her body will not be able to absorb necessary nutrients and immune system function will be severely decreased. This puts the person at a much higher risk for other disorders, including auto immune diseases such as Crohn's disease, lupus, and Type I diabetes, as well as cancer and osteoporosis. Fortunately, if a person with celiac disease eats a 100% gluten-free diet, his or her risk of these disorders decreases to equal the risk of the general population.

What to Avoid

Grains and grain products that must be avoided include:

- Wheat, including the varieties of: Durum, Spelt, Kamut, Einkorn, Emmer, Graham
- Cracked Wheat
- Bulgur
- Wheat bran
- Wheat germ
- Wheat germ oil
- Wheat starch
- Cream of Wheat
- Farina
- Couscous
- Pastas made from wheat, matzo, seitan, or semolina flours
- Barley, including malt
- Rye
- Triticale (hybrid grain of rye and wheat)
- Oats, in some cases

Note: Oats are not in the same taxonomical tribe as wheat, rye, and barley, but in some cases celiac individuals have an intestinal response towards oats. The celiac response may sometimes be related to contamination with wheat in the field or factory, such as during crop rotation, processing, or storage in a grain elevator. However, even certified, 100% gluten-free oats still cause a celiac reaction in certain people with celiac disease, and long-term effects are not well-studied for any celiac consuming oats on a regular basis. Therefore, none of the recipes in this book include any oats or oat flours.

Cooking Gluten-Free

Finding out that you have celiac disease or choosing to eat a gluten-free diet may thrust you into cooking whether you enjoy cooking or not. Although many foods become restricted, it is helpful to focus on the many foods that are naturally gluten-free. Below is a list showing just a small sampling of the thousands of foods that are naturally gluten-free, and you can probably think of many more. For descriptions and more information about the grains and legumes in this list, see pages 184–187.

Gluten-free Foods

Grains	Carrots	**All Fruits**	Goose	Mussels
Amaranth	Cauliflower	Apples	Lamb	Oysters
Buckwheat	Cucumbers	Apricots	Pork	Salmon
Corn	Green Beans	Bananas	Turkey	Shrimp
Millet	Onions	Cantaloupe		Tilapia
Quinoa	Peppers	Cherries	**All Dairy**	Trout
Rice	Pumpkins	Grapefruit	**Products**	Tuna
Sorghum	Squash	Grapes	**(unprocessed)**	Walleye
Teff	Tomatoes	Lemons	Buttermilk	
Wild Rice		Limes	Cheese	**All Herbs**
	All Legumes	Mangoes	Cottage Cheese	**All Eggs**
Roots	Black Beans	Oranges	Cream	
Arrowroot	Black-eye Peas	Peaches	Cream Cheese	**All Nuts and**
Cassava	Kidney Beans	Plums	Milk	**Seeds**
Potatoes	Lentils	Pears	Yogurt	Almonds
Rutabaga	Lima Beans	Watermelon		Cashews
Sweet Potatoes	Navy Beans		**All Natural**	Hazelnuts
Tapioca	Peanuts	**All Natural**	**Fish/Shellfish**	Hickory Nuts
	Pinto Beans	**Meats/Poultry**	Catfish	Pecans
All Vegetables	Soybeans	Beef	Clams	Pistachios
Beets	Split Peas	Chicken	Cod	Sunflower Seeds
Broccoli	Sweet Peas	Duck	Halibut	Walnuts

Don't be Surprised by Gluten in Unexpected Places

Many products containing gluten may surprise you, and it's not always easy to interpret the label of food products. Gluten can be "hiding" in unexpected places. Here is a list of products you should always avoid:
• Grain alcohol such as beer, ale, whisky, rye, scotch, bourbon, and grain vodka
• Malt or Malt Flavoring (made from barley) or malt vinegar

• Vital wheat gluten (common in soy products)
• Anything in bulk bins, common at natural food stores. Cross-contamination can easily occur and these foods are not considered gluten-free. Only buy flours or grains that are packaged in air-tight packaging.
• Any gluten-free foods that are made in the same plant or with the same equipment as gluten-containing products.

Carefully read the food package for a list of common allergens, and call the company if in doubt.
• Pans, toasters, panini presses, grills, other kitchen appliances, and kitchen surfaces that have been used with gluten-containing foods. Always use separate equipment and utensils for gluten-free foods.

Call to be Sure

If you see this ingredient in a product, call the company and ask if the product is gluten-free. For more information about reading labels, see page 188.

Artificial flavorings	Hydrolyzed protein
Caramel colorings or flavorings	Natural flavorings
	Preservatives
Cereal fillers	Semolina
Colorings	Starch
Curry Powder	Soy Sauce
Dextrins	Spices
Extracts	Textured vegetable
Flavorings	protein (TVP)
Maltodextrin	Vegetable gum
Modified starch	Vegetable protein
Modified food starch	Vinegar

About Gluten-Free Pasta

There are many gluten-free pastas available on the market. While the shapes may look like wheat pasta, gluten-free pastas are made from corn, quinoa, rice, or other gluten-free grains. Each time you cook pasta, carefully follow the directions on the package.

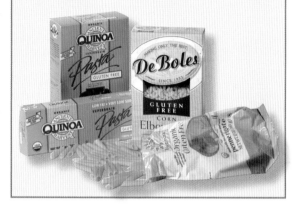

Gluten-Free All-Purpose Flours, Flour Mixes, Grain Flours, and Meals

There are many gluten-free all-purpose flour mixes, cookie and cake mixes, and other flour-based mixes on the market. Each all-purpose flour mix is slightly different. Some are made with bean flour, while others contain tapioca or rice flour. Every one has a different combination of ingredients so it will yield different results. That is why when our recipes call for all-purpose flour we specify which brand of flour we have used. If you do not use that specific brand of flour, your recipe may not be successful. Sometimes you can substitute another brand and it will work, but we have found that the quantity needed varies greatly along with taste, texture, and cooking time.

Pure meals such as cornmeal or pure flours such as rice flour or tapioca flour should be interchangeable from brand to brand.

All of the flours that we have used in the recipes in this book are readily available in stores or online. For a complete list of resources with addresses, see page 210.

Examples of gluten-free all-purpose flour mixes:

- Arrowhead Mills® Gluten-free All purpose Baking Mix
- Bob's Red Mill® All-Purpose Gluten-free Baking Flour
- Domata Living® Flour
- Jules® All Purpose Gluten-free Flour
- King Arthur® Gluten-free Multi-Purpose Flour
- Kinnikinnick® All-Purpose Celiac Flour
- Namaste® Perfect Flour Blend
- Pamela's® Baking and Pancake Mix
- Tom Sawyer's® Gluten-free Flour

Specific Products That are Gluten-Free

There are many specific products on the market that are gluten-free, with more being developed every day. Many products that are gluten-free may not specifically be labeled as such. However, with the growing interest in gluten-free cooking, many manufacturers are now beginning to label products to indicate if they are gluten-free. While there are hundreds of gluten-free products available, here is a partial list of some of the products that are gluten-free at the time of this book's printing. This is not an endorsement of the products, but we have used most of these products when testing recipes for this book. We often suggest these specific brands when calling for a product in the recipe.

- Better Than Bouillon®
- Cookies® Original BBQ Sauce
- Cool Whip® Whipped Topping
- Corn Chex®
- All Crisco® products
- Daisy® Sour Cream
- Dei Fratelli® Pizza Sauce
- Dickinson's® Lemon Curd
- French's® Mustard
- Heinz® Tomato Ketchup

- Hellmann's®/Best Foods® Real Mayonnaise
- Hormel® Miniature Pepperoni Slices
- Hormel® Cure 81® Ham
- Hunts® Traditional Spaghetti Sauce
- Jell-O® Gelatin
- Jif® Peanut Butter
- John Morrell® Beef Franks
- Johnsonville® Breakfast Links
- Kraft® Philadelphia® Cream Cheese

- Kraft® Velveeta®
- Kinnikinnick® Panko-style Bread Crumbs
- Knox® Gelatin
- Kraft® American Singles
- La Choy® Lite Soy Sauce
- Log Cabin® Pancake Syrup (Original and Lite)
- McCormick® Cocktail Sauce
- Nature's Path® Gorilla Munch® Cereal
- Nestlé® Toll House® Cocoa

- Nestlé® Toll House® Semi-Sweet Morsels (regular size)
- Newman's Own® Oil and Vinegar Salad Dressing
- Pace® Picante Sauce
- Pam® Original Non-Stick Cooking Spray
- Rice Chex®
- Skippy® Peanut Butter
- Snickers® Candy Bar
- Tabasco® Pepper Sauce
- V8®

Double Check the Ingredients

Whenever you are unsure of a product or if it is not clearly marked as gluten-free, double-check the ingredients. Here are some foods and other products that you might not think to check before using:

Alcohol	Cosmetics	Marinades	Shampoos
Anything thickened or creamy	Curry powder	Mayonnaise	Soaps
Bacon	Deli meat	Medications	Soups
Baked beans	Detergent	Mouthwash	Soy Sauce
Baking powder	Envelopes	Mustard	Spices
Barbecue sauce	Glues/pastes	Pancake syrup	Stamps
Beer	Gravy	Pickles	Stickers
Blue cheese	Ham	Pie fillings	Sunscreen
Bouillon	Hot dogs	Pizza sauce	Toothpaste
Breakfast cereals, such as puffed rice cereal	Ice cream	Play-doh®	Vegetable nonstick cooking sprays
	Imitation fish or crab	Processed cheese	
	Imitation meat products for vegetarians	Processed meat	Vinegar
Broth		Puddings	Vitamins
Candy	Ketchup	Reduced-fat products	Whipped topping
Cocoa	Lip balm	Ready-made meals	Wine
Coffee, instant	Lipstick	Salad dressings	Yogurt
Communion wafers	Margarine	Sauces	
		Self-basting poultry	

Now you are ready to start cooking and enjoying so many of the foods that you have always loved. So grab the whisk, find the bowls, and turn on the oven, because you are about to have fun making delicious gluten-free foods that are easy, inexpensive, and most of all, good for you!

1 Main Dishes

1

Classic Beef Stroganoff 🄗🄟

Freeze for Later

These gluten-free noodles can be made ahead, dried, and then frozen. After cutting the noodles, let them dry on the cutting board for a few hours. Then seal them in a freezer bag and freeze for up to 3 months. When you need them, cook the frozen noodles as you would fresh ones.

Nutrition Per Serving:

680 calories, 37g fat, 17g saturated fat, 420mg cholesterol, 1270mg sodium, 53g carbohydrate, 4g fiber, 32g protein

Ingredients

1   pound beef tenderloin, cut ½ inch thick
2   tablespoons butter
½ pound fresh mushrooms, trimmed and sliced
½ cup chopped onion
1½ cups gluten-free beef broth such as Better Than Bouillon®
½ teaspoon salt
1   small clove garlic, minced
¼ cup cold water
2   tablespoons cornstarch
1   cup gluten-free dairy sour cream
1   recipe Gluten-Free Noodles

Directions

1 Cut meat across the grain into ½-inch-thick strips about 1½ inches long. In large skillet melt butter. Add mushrooms and onion; cook and stir until onion is tender. Remove from skillet. In same skillet cook meat until light brown. Stir in broth, salt, and garlic. Simmer, covered, for 15 minutes.

2 Mix cold water and cornstarch; stir into broth mixture. Add mushrooms and onion. Bring to boiling, stirring constantly. Boil and stir for 1 minute. Reduce heat. Stir in sour cream; heat through. Serve over hot cooked Gluten-Free Noodles. Serve immediately. *Serves 6.*

Gluten-Free Noodles

1 In a small bowl mix together 1 cup all-purpose gluten-free flour such as Domata Living™ Flour and 1 teaspoon salt. Make a well in center of mixture. Add 1 egg, 2 egg yolks, and 2 tablespoons carbonated water. Using 2 to 4 tablespoons water, mix in just enough to make a soft round ball. See Photo A.

2 Place on a flour-covered board and let rest for 10 minutes. Divide into four portions. See Photo B.

3 Using a rolling pin, roll each portion into a rectangle about ⅛ inch thick. See Photo C. Roll and cut into ¼-inch strips. Unroll dough. See Photo D. Repeat with remaining dough. To cook noodles, fill a large saucepan with 6 cups water and 1 teaspoon salt. Bring to rolling boil. Add noodles; cook about 5 minutes or until tender. Do not overcook. Drain in a strainer. Makes 3 to 4 cups cooked noodles.

A   B   C

What's on the Menu:
- Classic Beef Stroganoff
- Scalloped Corn (see page 54)
- Blue Cheese Veggies (see page 72)

Rich gluten-free egg noodles are the star in this classic main dish that's easy to make for a special occasion or any night of the week.

D

1

Add a Flavor Variation

Substitute fresh asparagus or fresh green beans for the pea pods. They will cook in about the same amount of time.

Read the Label

There are many gluten-free pastas available. They can be made from corn, quinoa, rice, and other gluten-free grains. When cooking these pastas, read the instructions carefully. Overcooking can make the pasta fall apart or become gummy.

The green pea pods and the penne pasta make this easy dish both pretty and delicious.

Nutrition Per Serving:
519 calories, 12g fat, 3g saturated fat, 93mg cholesterol, 394 mg sodium, 62g carbohydrate, 9g fiber, 41g protein

Lemon Chicken with Pea Pods **HP** **EF**

Ingredients

- 2 8-ounce packages gluten-free penne pasta or similar pasta
- 2 tablespoons canola oil
- 3 to 4 skinless, boneless chicken breasts, cut into 1-inch pieces
- 1 cup frozen pea pods cut into pieces
- ½ teaspoon garlic salt
- ½ cup grated Parmesan cheese
- ¼ cup lemon juice
- 2 tablespoons chopped fresh parsley (optional)
  Finely shredded Parmesan cheese

Directions

1 In a large pot cook pasta as directed on package. Drain and pour pasta into a large bowl. Cover with foil and set aside.

2 In a large skillet heat oil on medium heat. Add chicken and cook about 6 minutes or until tender. Transfer cooked chicken to bowl with pasta.

3 In the same skillet add pea pods and garlic salt. Cook and stir for 1 minute. Transfer to bowl with chicken and pasta. Add ½ cup grated cheese, lemon juice, and, if desired, parsley; toss to combine. Sprinkle with finely shredded cheese. Serve immediately. *Serves 6.*

Fish Tacos 🅗🅟 🅦🅖

Ingredients

1 pound fresh or frozen skinless white fish such as cod

2 tablespoons butter, softened

½ teaspoon sea salt

¼ teaspoon onion powder

3 tablespoons gluten-free mayonnaise such as Hellmann's®/ Best Foods® Real Mayonnaise

1 tablespoon lemon juice

1½ cups packaged coleslaw mix or shredded cabbage

8 corn taco shells, warmed

1 recipe Mango-Pepper Salsa

Directions

1 Thaw fish, if frozen. Rinse and pat dry. Preheat oven to 400°F. Grease a shallow baking pan. Set aside. Cut fish into 1-inch pieces. Place in prepared baking pan. In a small bowl combine butter, salt, and onion powder. Brush over fish. Bake about 8 minutes or until fish flakes easily with a fork.

2 In a medium bowl stir together mayonnaise and lemon juice. Add coleslaw mix and toss lightly. Spoon mixture into taco shells. Add fish pieces and top with Mango-Pepper Salsa. *Serves 4.*

Mango-Pepper Salsa

1 In a small bowl combine 1½ cups chopped, peeled mangoes, ¾ cup finely chopped red sweet pepper, ¼ cup thinly sliced green onions, 2 tablespoons lemon juice, 1 tablespoon olive oil, ½ teaspoon black pepper, and ¼ teaspoon sea salt. Makes 2 cups.

Note: For tips on cutting mangoes, see page 190.

Make Ahead and Save Time
Make up a batch of the Mango-Pepper Salsa and store it in a small glass jar in the refrigerator. It will keep for up to 3 days. This salsa is also great on chicken or pork.

Purchased corn tacos shells take on new flavor when filled with crunchy cabbage slaw, flaky white fish, and zesty salsa.

Nutrition Per Serving:
402 calories, 21g fat, 5g saturated fat, 62mg cholesterol, 803 mg sodium, 31g carbohydrate, 4g fiber, 23g protein

Main Dishes

Potato-Egg Bake Ⓥ ⒽⓅ

y

Special Health Benefits

Eggs provide protein, vitamin D, and choline, all essential nutrients. Spinach provides folic acid and calcium.

Add a Flavor Variation

Kick the flavor up a notch with jalapeño peppers. Wearing plastic gloves,

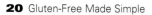

finely chop the peppers and add 1 tablespoon to the mixture.

The Cost:

Eggs are a great value. On average they cost about 11¢ each. The cost of this entire recipe is about $3.00.

Nutrition Per Serving:
160 calories, 8g fat, 3g saturated fat, 205mg cholesterol, 460 mg sodium, 11g carbohydrate, 1g fiber, 10g protein

Ingredients

8 eggs
¾ cup whole milk
2½ cups frozen shredded potatoes
¾ cup shredded cheddar cheese
½ cup chopped fresh spinach
½ cup cubed gluten-free ham (optional)
1 tablespoon chopped green sweet pepper
1 tablespoon chopped red sweet pepper
1 teaspoon salt
1 teaspoon chopped fresh chives
½ teaspoon black pepper
¾ cup shredded cheddar cheese

Directions

1 Preheat oven to 325°F. Grease a 5-cup shallow baking dish. Set aside. In a small mixing bowl beat eggs with a whisk until well blended and frothy. Beat in milk. See Photo A. Set aside.

2 In a large mixing bowl combine potatoes, ¾ cup cheese, spinach, ham (if desired), green and red sweet pepper, salt, chives, and black pepper. Mix well. See Photo B.

3 Add egg mixture to potato mixture and mix well. See Photo C.

4 Pour into the prepared baking dish. Sprinkle with ¾ cup cheese. See Photo D. Bake about 45 minutes or until mixture is set and knife comes out clean when inserted in the center. Serve immediately. *Serves 9.*

A

B

C

D

y

w

Eggs combine with shredded potatoes in this egg casserole that's wonderful for a weekend brunch. Bits of red and green pepper and fresh spinach add just the right amount of extra flavor.

What's on the Menu:
- Potato-Egg Bake
- Breakfast Sausages (see page 175)
- Fresh Fruit

Thai Chicken Pasta HP CF EF

*Most of the prep
time for this main
dish comes from
measuring spices.
Mix the brown
sugar, lemon juice,
and spices ahead of
time and keep them
refrigerated until
ready to cook.*

Peanut butter
partners with an
array of spices to
capture the unique
flavor of Thai
cooking in this main
dish favorite.

Ingredients

3 skinless, boneless
chicken breasts

2 red and/or green
sweet peppers,
chopped

1 fresh jalapeño pepper,
chopped

1 cup water

¾ cup gluten-free peanut
butter

¾ cup gluten-free light
soy sauce such as
La Choy® Lite

½ cup olive oil

3 tablespoons packed
brown sugar

3 tablespoons lemon
juice

½ teaspoon ground
ginger

½ teaspoon dried cilantro

½ teaspoon crushed red
pepper

2 8-ounce packages
gluten-free spaghetti

½ cup peanuts

Directions

1 Preheat oven to 350°F. Cut chicken into 1-inch
pieces. In a 13x9-inch baking pan combine
chicken, sweet peppers, and jalapeño pepper; add
water. Cover with foil. Bake about 25 minutes or
until chicken is tender. Drain chicken mixture and
place in a small bowl. Set aside.

2 For sauce, in a small saucepan mix peanut butter,
soy sauce, and oil until smooth. Stir in brown
sugar, lemon juice, ginger, cilantro, and crushed
red pepper. Cook on medium-low heat for
1 minute. Stir in most of the chicken mixture;
cook for 1 minute more.

3 Cook pasta as directed on package. Drain well.
Spoon sauce on cooked pasta. Top with remaining
chicken mixture and peanuts. Serve immediately.
Serves 6.

Carol says:

Try using this spicy, peanut butter
sauce on a variety of foods. Serve
over any type of pasta, cooked
rice, or steamed vegetables.

**Nutrition
Per Serving:**
670 calories, 44g
fat, 8g saturated fat,
85mg cholesterol,
1330mg sodium,
24g carbohydrate,
4g fiber, 48g protein

Macaroni and Cheese ⓥ Ⓗ︎Ⓟ Ⓔ︎Ⓕ

Ingredients

- 1 8-ounce package gluten-free macaroni
- 3 tablespoons butter
- 1 small onion, chopped
- ¼ cup chopped green sweet pepper
- 1 teaspoon salt
- ¼ teaspoon dry mustard
- 2 cups milk
- 1 tablespoon cornstarch
- 1½ cups shredded sharp cheddar cheese
- 1 cup buttered, toasted gluten-free bread crumbs (optional)

Directions

1 Preheat oven to 400°F. Grease a 1½-quart shallow baking dish. Set aside.

2 Cook macaroni as directed on package. Drain well. Place cooked macaroni in prepared baking dish.

3 In a medium skillet melt butter. Add onion and green pepper; cook until tender. Stir in salt and dry mustard. In a small bowl mix ¼ cup of the milk and cornstarch. Gradually stir cornstarch mixture and the remaining milk into onion mixture. Cook and stir until thickened, about 2 minutes. Add cheese, stirring until just melted. Pour mixture over macaroni in baking dish and mix well. If desired, top with bread crumbs.

4 Bake about 20 minutes or until bubbly. Serve immediately. *Serves 6.*

The Cost
Macaroni and cheese has always been an economical meal. Even when using more expensive gluten-free pasta, the cost of this main dish is still only about $4.50, or 75¢ per serving.

Love macaroni and cheese? Don't give it up because you're eating gluten-free. This recipe makes it easy to enjoy this famous family pleaser.

Nutrition Per Serving:
400 calories, 18g fat, 10g saturated fat, 45mg cholesterol, 510 mg sodium, 47g carbohydrate, 5g fiber, 14g protein

1

Add a Flavor Variation

There are dozens of possibilities for pizza toppings, but did you know you can also boost the flavor of the crust? Add one of these options to the dry ingredients:

- *1 tablespoon chopped fresh basil*
- *2 teaspoons chopped fresh chives*
- *1 teaspoon dried oregano*

Nutrition Per Serving:
290 calories, 9g fat, 4g saturated fat, 55mg cholesterol, 960mg sodium, 36g carbohydrate, 3g fiber, 16g protein

---

Veggie Pizza Ⓥ ⒽⓅ

Ingredients

1¼ cups gluten-free all-purpose flour such as Domata Living™ Flour

¼ cup yellow cornmeal

1 tablespoon sugar

1 teaspoon salt

¾ cup water

1 egg

1¼ teaspoons olive oil

1 cup gluten-free pizza sauce such as Dei Fratelli® Prima Qualita Pizza Sauce

¾ cup chopped fresh tomatoes

½ cup sliced canned artichokes, drained

2 cups shredded Italian blend cheese

Fresh spinach leaves

Other suggested toppings:

Fresh pineapple

Sliced red or green sweet peppers

Gluten-free green or black olives

Onions

Directions

1 Preheat oven to 400°F. In a medium mixing bowl combine flour, cornmeal, sugar, and salt. Make a well in the middle of the dry ingredients. In a glass measuring cup combine water, egg, and oil. Add egg mixture to dry ingredients and mix well. See Photo A.

2 Place dough on a greased 14-inch pizza pan. Using your fingers, push the dough to the edge of the pan. See Photo B. Using a fork, make holes in the dough. See Photo C. Bake crust for 12 minutes. Remove from oven.

3 Spread crust with pizza sauce. Add chopped tomatoes and artichokes. Sprinkle with cheese. Top with spinach. Return to oven and bake for about 10 more minutes or until cheese is bubbly. *Serves 4.*

Elizabeth says:

The sugar in this gluten-free crust helps it brown. The pizza crust is delicious and crisp but may not brown as much as a wheat flour crust.

A B C

Artichokes, tomatoes, spinach, or just cheese—all taste great on this crisp gluten-free pizza crust.

What's on the Menu:
- Veggie Pizza
- Easy Cabbage Salad (see page 62)
- Mango-Peach Smoothie (see page 139)

1

Read the Label

Most soy sauces contain wheat, so be sure to read the label. For a list of some brand-name products that are gluten-free see page 13.

Special Health Benefits

Brown rice contains the whole kernel of rice. Therefore it has more fiber, B vitamins, and other essential nutrients than white rice products.

Nutrition Per Serving:
440 calories, 12g fat, 3g saturated fat, 150mg cholesterol, 490 mg sodium, 48g carbohydrate, 4g fiber, 33g protein

---

Fried Rice with Fish **HP** **CF** **WG**

Ingredients

1 pound fresh or frozen white fish such as halibut or cod

2 tablespoons butter, softened

½ teaspoon garlic salt

½ teaspoon coarse pepper

2 eggs

Salt and pepper

2 tablespoons butter

3 tablespoons olive oil

½ cup shredded carrot

¼ cup chopped celery

¼ cup chopped green beans or asparagus

2 tablespoons chopped green onion

4 cups cold cooked brown rice

2 tablespoons gluten-free light soy sauce such as La Choy® Lite

Mango slices (optional)

Cashews (optional)

Directions

1 Thaw fish, if frozen. Rinse and pat dry. Preheat oven to 400°F. Cut fish into 1½-inch pieces. Place in a greased shallow baking pan. In a small bowl combine 2 tablespoons softened butter, garlic salt, and ½ teaspoon pepper. Brush over fish. Bake about 8 minutes or until fish flakes easily with a fork.

2 Meanwhile, in a small bowl beat eggs, salt, and more pepper. In a large skillet melt 2 tablespoons butter. Add egg mixture. Turn eggs over to be sure they are completely cooked. See Photo A. Remove eggs from pan by sliding them out onto a clean cutting board. See Photo B.

3 Roll up eggs and cut into thin strips. See Photo C. Place eggs in small bowl; cover to keep warm.

4 In the same skillet heat olive oil. Add carrot, celery, asparagus, and green onion; cook on high heat about 5 minutes or until tender, stirring occasionally. Stir in brown rice and soy sauce and cook until heated through. Stir in egg strips.

5 Arrange cooked fish and rice mixture on a platter. If desired, garnish with mango slices and cashews. *Serves 4.*

A   B   C

What's on the Menu:
- Fried Rice with Fish
- Key Lime Mousse (see page 152)

Wholesome brown rice combines with healthy vegetables and eggs to make this flavorful and good-for-you dish.

Plan Ahead

Save time by preparing the peppers ahead of time. Cover and refrigerate them until ready to cook.

Read the Label

Any time you purchase a premade sauce read the label carefully. Although most high-quality spaghetti sauces are gluten-free, some with cheese or meat may not be. If in doubt, and the label doesn't say "gluten-free," call the company or check on the company's web site to be sure.

Stuffed Peppers ⓛⒻ ⒽⓅ ⒺⒻ

Ingredients

4   medium green, yellow, or red sweet peppers
1   pound ground beef
1   cup cooked rice
1   cup gluten-free spaghetti sauce such as Hunts®Traditional Spaghetti Sauce
1   teaspoon dried oregano or 2 teaspoons chopped fresh oregano
1   teaspoon chopped fresh chives
1   teaspoon celery seed
¾   cup shredded Parmesan cheese

Directions

1 Preheat oven to 350°F. Lightly grease an 8x8-inch baking pan. Set aside.

2 Using a sharp knife, remove tops of peppers. See Photo A. Using a spoon, remove the seeds and membranes. See Photo B. Place peppers in a large pot and add 5 cups salted water. See Photo C. Bring to boiling and boil for 5 minutes. Remove peppers from pan and drain well. Cool slightly.

3 In a medium skillet brown ground beef. Drain beef. Transfer beef to a medium bowl. Add rice, half of the spaghetti sauce, oregano, chives, and celery seed. Mix well.

4 Stuff peppers with beef mixture. See Photo D. Top with remaining spaghetti sauce and cheese. Place in the prepared baking pan. Cover with foil and bake for 45 minutes. Uncover and bake for 15 minutes more.

Nutrition per Serving:
270 calories, 7g fat, 2g saturated fat, 60mg cholesterol, 90 mg sodium, 27g carbohydrate, 4g fiber, 25g protein

A

B

C

D

Loaded with beef and rice, these colorful peppers are simple to make. If you prepare the peppers ahead of time, all you have to do at the last minute is stuff the peppers and pop them in the oven.

What's on the Menu:
- Stuffed Peppers
- Apple Walnut Salad (see page 71)
- Millet Flatbread (see page 84)

Spaghetti and Meatballs 🄛🄵 🄷🄿

Ingredients

1 cup Rice Chex®
1 pound ground beef
2 eggs, beaten
2 teaspoons dried minced onion
1 teaspoon dried oregano
½ cup instant white rice
1 teaspoon sea salt
½ teaspoon pepper
1 recipe Spaghetti Sauce
2 8-ounce packages gluten-free spaghetti
Grated and/or shredded Parmesan cheese

Directions

1 To crush the Rice Chex, place cereal in a plastic bag. Use a rolling pin to crush the cereal. See page 36 for tips on crushing cereal.

2 In a large mixing bowl mix together ground beef, eggs, onion, and oregano. See Photo A.

3 Add uncooked rice, salt, and pepper. Add the crushed cereal. Mix well. See Photo B. Cover and refrigerate for 1 hour.

4 Preheat oven to 350°F. Form meat mixture into sixteen 1½-inch meatballs. Place in a shallow baking pan, leaving about 1 inch between the meatballs. See Photo C. Bake for 30 minutes. Meanwhile, prepare Spaghetti Sauce.

5 Cook pasta as directed on package. Drain well. Serve pasta with meatballs and sauce. Garnish with cheese. Serve immediately. *Serves 8.*

Spaghetti Sauce

1 In a large saucepan heat 1 tablespoon olive oil. Add 1 small onion, chopped, and 1 small clove garlic, minced, and cook until tender.

2 Stir in one 28-ounce can crushed tomatoes, one 15-ounce can tomato sauce, one 14.5-ounce can undrained diced tomatoes or 1½ cups peeled and diced fresh tomatoes, 1 tablespoon sugar, 1 tablespoon quick-cooking tapioca, 1 tablespoon grated Parmesan cheese, 1 teaspoon dried oregano, and 1 teaspoon dried basil. Simmer, covered, for 20 minutes. Add salt and pepper to taste.

Freeze for Later

Make the meatballs ahead and place them in a tightly covered freezer container. Freeze for up to 3 months. When ready to cook, thaw the meatballs in the refrigerator and bake as directed.

1

Marcia says:

I really missed eating spaghetti and meatballs—this delicious recipe is now a weeknight dinner favorite.

Nutrition Per Serving:

383 calories, 4g fat, 1g saturated fat, 85mg cholesterol, 872mg sodium, 65g carbohydrate, 9g fiber, 20g protein

A   B   C

What's on the Menu:
- Spaghetti and Meatballs
- Greek Salad (see page 58)
- Feta-Basil Bread (see page 82)

Who doesn't love spaghetti and meatballs? With just a few minor changes to a favorite recipe, it's now gluten-free. Enjoy!

Salmon Cakes

The Cost

Using canned salmon makes these cakes an inexpensive meal. The cost of the recipe is about $4.00, or about $1.00 per serving.

Add a Flavor Variation

Cook some fresh or frozen peas and add them to a gluten-free white sauce (see page 194). Serve the creamy sauce over the cakes.

For a scrumptious last-minute meal, keep the ingredients for this recipe on your pantry shelf. Dinner will be ready in almost no time.

Ingredients

½ cup Rice Chex®
1 14.75-ounce can salmon
2 eggs, beaten
¼ cup whole milk
1 tablespoon sliced green onion
1 teaspoon sugar
1 teaspoon quick-cooking tapioca
1 teaspoon chopped fresh dill
½ teaspoon salt
½ teaspoon pepper
¼ cup olive oil
Lemon wedges

Directions

1 To crush the Rice Chex, place cereal in a plastic bag. Use a rolling pin to crush the cereal. See page 36 for tips on crushing cereal.

2 Remove and discard all bones and skin from salmon. Drain salmon, reserving ⅓ cup liquid. In a large mixing bowl combine crushed cereal, salmon, reserved salmon liquid, eggs, milk, onion, sugar, tapioca, dill, salt, and pepper. Mix well. Cover and refrigerate for 15 minutes.

3 Form salmon mixture into 8 small patties. Mixture will be very soft. In a medium skillet heat olive oil. Add patties and cook until golden brown on both sides. Cook for 5 minutes more. Serve immediately with lemon wedges. *Serves 4.*

Nutrition Per Serving:

230 calories, 14g fat, 3g saturated fat, 175mg cholesterol, 790 mg sodium, 3g carbohydrate, 0g fiber, 24g protein

Cheesy Scalloped Potatoes ⓗⓟ ⓔⓕ

Ingredients

1 tablespoon onion

1 tablespoon chopped fresh chives

1 tablespoon chopped fresh parsley

¼ cup butter

¼ cup cold water

2 tablespoons cornstarch

2 cups milk

Salt and pepper

6 large potatoes such as russet or Yukon gold

¾ cup shredded cheddar cheese

¼ cup diced gluten-free ham

Directions

1 Preheat oven to 350°F. Grease a 2-quart shallow baking dish. Set aside.

2 For sauce, in a medium saucepan cook onion, chives, and parsley in butter until tender. In a small bowl mix water and cornstarch; stir into onion mixture. Gradually stir in milk. Cook and stir on medium heat until thickened. Cook for 1 more minute. Add salt and pepper to taste.

3 Alternately layer potatoes, cheese, ham, and sauce in the prepared baking dish. Cover with foil and bake for 30 minutes. Uncover and bake for 1 hour more. *Serves 6.*

Special Health Benefits

Whether you prefer red potatoes, Yukon gold, or russets, humble potatoes pack a great deal of nutrition. They are high in potassium and vitamin C.

The Cost

Potatoes are a great value—especially when you buy them in large-quantity bags. The cost of this entire recipe is about $3.50. That makes each serving less than 60¢ each.

The captivating aroma of these potatoes baking will bring the whole family to the dinner table the first time you call.

Nutrition Per Serving:
350 calories, 10g fat, 6g saturated fat, 30mg cholesterol, 680mg sodium, 51g carbohydrate, 4g fiber, 14g protein

Stuffed Pork Chops ⓗⓟ ⓔⓕ

Freeze for Later

Purchase the pork chops and slice as shown so they are ready to stuff. Seal them in freezer bags. Make the stuffing and place it in a separate freezer container. Freeze both the chops and the stuffing for up to 1 month. When ready to cook, thaw both chops and stuffing in the refrigerator. Then prepare as directed.

Nutrition Per Serving:
270 calories, 13g fat, 2g saturated fat, 35mg cholesterol, 450 mg sodium, 26g carbohydrate, 2g fiber, 12g protein

Ingredients

2 butterfly pork chops, cut 2 inches thick (about 1 pound each)
1 cup Buttery Corn Bread cut into small pieces (see page 81)
½ cup finely chopped apple
¼ cup finely chopped celery
2 tablespoons chopped green onion
2 teaspoons chopped fresh sage or 1 teaspoon dried sage
¼ cup finely chopped walnuts
¼ cup golden raisins
1 teaspoon salt
½ teaspoon pepper
¼ cup olive oil
4 fresh apricots, sliced
Fresh sage leaves

Directions

1 Preheat oven to 350°F. Grease a shallow baking dish. Set aside. Using a sharp knife, cut the butterfly pork chops in half. See Photo A. Using a smaller knife, make a pocket in the side of each piece. See Photo B. Set aside.

2 In a medium bowl stir together Buttery Corn Bread pieces, apple, celery, onion, and chopped or dried sage. Add walnuts, raisins, salt, and pepper. Mix well. Stuff the mixture into the pockets of the pork chops. See Photo C.

3 In a large skillet heat oil. Add pork chops and brown on both sides. Transfer to prepared baking dish. Top with apricots and sage leaves. Cover with foil and bake about 50 minutes or until chops are thoroughly cooked. Serve immediately. *Serves 4.*

> **Elizabeth says:**
> The gluten-free corn bread creates a stuffing with the perfect texture—it's neither soggy nor too dry.

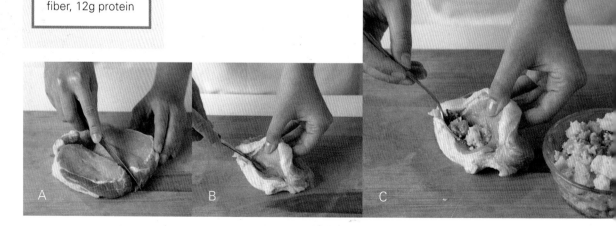

Apricots and sage add delightful flavor to these corn bread-stuffed pork chops that the whole family will love.

What's on the Menu:
- Stuffed Pork Chops
- Sweet Potato Fries (see page 52)
- Easy Cabbage Salad (see page 62)

Old-Fashioned Meat Loaf (HP) (CF)

1

Special Health Benefits

Beef and eggs combine to provide protein, zinc, iron, and choline to help the immune system.

Read the Label

Not all corn cereals are gluten-free. Corn Chex® is certified to be gluten-free, as its label specifies.

The Cost

This gluten-free meat loaf makes a relatively inexpensive meal. The cost of one serving is about 75¢.

Ingredients

⅔ cup Corn Chex®

1½ pounds ground beef

1 cup cooked white or brown rice

2 eggs

3 tablespoons gluten-free ketchup such as Heinz® Tomato Ketchup

1 teaspoon dried parsley

1 teaspoon finely chopped onion

½ teaspoon salt

¼ teaspoon pepper

⅓ cup gluten-free ketchup such as Heinz® Tomato Ketchup

2 tablespoons packed brown sugar

Directions

1 Place the Corn Chex in a plastic bag. Use a rolling pin to crush the cereal. See Photo A. Set aside.

2 In a large bowl combine ground beef, rice, eggs, 3 tablespoons ketchup, parsley, onion, salt, and pepper. Add crushed cereal. Mix well. See Photo B.

3 Shape the meat mixture into 2 small loaves. Place on a baking sheet. See Photo C.

4 In a small bowl mix ⅓ cup ketchup and brown sugar. Spoon half of the mixture over each loaf. See Photo D. Bake for 45 minutes. *Serves 6.*

Carol says:

The crushed Corn Chex® cereal replaces the cracker or bread crumbs often found in traditional meat loaf recipes, acting as a binder for all of the ingredients.

Nutrition Per Serving:
230 calories, 7g fat, 2g saturated fat, 130mg cholesterol, 18g carbohydrate, 0g fiber, 25g protein

A

B

C

D

What's on the Menu:
- Old-Fashioned Meat Loaf
- Wild Rice Casserole (see page 46)
- Broiled Tomatoes (see page 64)

Add a side dish of mashed potatoes or steamed carrots and you have the perfect comfort food meal—no gluten necessary!

In this chapter we have given you some sample menu ideas using many of the recipes in the book. Choosing a menu for you or your family when you are eating gluten-free may seem like a big task. But it is really quite easy if you keep these things in mind:

- Choose a protein for each meal such as meat, eggs, or beans.
- Choose a starch for each meal such as rice, potatoes, or a gluten-free bread.
- Always have at least one or two vegetables and fruits at each meal.
- Be sure and include dairy at each meal. Drink a glass of skim milk or add cheese or cottage cheese to the menu.
- Avoid processed or prepackaged foods that often contain gluten and add little nutrition to your menu.
- Do not add empty calories at a meal such as drinking soda.
- Oftentimes a casserole will give you protein, starch, vegetable, and dairy. Simply add a salad or fruit and the meal is complete.

Carol says:
When we developed these gluten-free recipes, we created them with real families in mind, knowing that planning a menu can be a challenge when you are learning to eat in a different way. We developed recipes that had easy-to-find ingredients and simple cooking methods so that making a meal would be enjoyable and easy to do.

2 Grains and Side Dishes

2

Three-Bean Bake LF HP CF EF

Freeze for Later

Bacon can be cooked and frozen so it's ready to use whenever you like. Simply cook bacon strips, drain them on paper towels, and place the strips in a shallow freezer container. Label and freeze for up to 3 months.

The Cost

Beans are a thrifty way to get plenty of protein and fiber. The cost for this entire recipe is about $4.00.

No potluck is complete without this classic. The molasses and bacon make it a crowd pleaser.

Ingredients

2 tablespoons canola oil

1 large onion, coarsely chopped

1 tablespoon dry mustard

1½ teaspoons dried thyme

1 15.8-ounce can red kidney beans, rinsed and drained

1 15.8-ounce can black beans, rinsed and drained

1 15-ounce can cannellini (white kidney) beans, rinsed and drained

¾ cup gluten-free ketchup such Heinz® Tomato Ketchup

¼ cup gluten-free apple cider vinegar

⅓ cup dark molasses

½ cup water

5 bacon slices, cooked

1 teaspoon gluten-free hot pepper sauce such as Tabasco®

Directions

1 Preheat oven to 350°F. In a large skillet heat oil over medium heat. Add onion and cook about 5 minutes or until almost tender. Add dry mustard and thyme and cook and stir for 1 minute. Transfer to a large bowl. Add all the beans, ketchup, vinegar, molasses, and water.

2 Pour into greased 2-quart baking dish; cover and bake for 45 minutes, stirring occasionally and adding more water if mixture seems dry. Crumble about 2 slices of the bacon. Stir crumbled bacon and hot pepper sauce into beans. Top with the remaining bacon slices. Bake 15 minutes longer. *Serves 8.*

Nutrition Per Serving:
345 calories, 7g fat, 1g saturated fat, 5mg cholesterol, 375 mg sodium, 57g carbohydrate, 14g fiber, 17g protein

Glazed Edamame (V) (HP) (CF) (EF)

Ingredients

½ cup water

24 ounces frozen, shelled edamame (do not thaw)

⅛ teaspoon salt

¼ cup canola oil

½ cup green onion, finely chopped

1 medium clove garlic, minced or pressed through a garlic press (about 2 teaspoons)

3 tablespoons finely chopped parsley leaves

3 tablespoons packed brown sugar

2 tablespoons gluten-free red wine vinegar

Directions

1 In a large skillet bring the water to a boil over high heat. Add the frozen edamame and salt; cover and cook until the beans have thawed (about 2 minutes).

2 Remove lid and cook about 2 minutes longer or until the water has evaporated and the edamame are heated through.

3 Add the oil, onions, and garlic; cook about 2 minutes or until the onions are soft. Remove from heat and stir in parsley, brown sugar, and vinegar. Serve immediately. *Serves 8.*

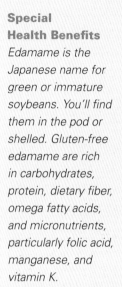

Special Health Benefits

Edamame is the Japanese name for green or immature soybeans. You'll find them in the pod or shelled. Gluten-free edamame are rich in carbohydrates, protein, dietary fiber, omega fatty acids, and micronutrients, particularly folic acid, manganese, and vitamin K.

Bored with the same old green beans and peas? Try this edamame recipe. Garlic, wine vinegar, and brown sugar give the tender beans incredible flavor.

Nutrition per serving:
179 calories, 11g fat, 1g saturated fat, 0mg cholesterol, 43 mg sodium, 13g carbohydrate, 4g fiber, 10g protein

Swiss Cheese Polenta Ⓥ ⓛⒻ ⒺⒻ ⓌⒼ

Special Health Benefits

A staple for centuries, corn is brimming with good-for-you nutrients, including carbohydrates, vitamins, and fiber.

The Cost

Cornmeal, which is naturally gluten-free, is easy on the budget. It comes in white, blue, or yellow varieties and all types are about the same price. The entire cost of this recipe is about $3.50 or less than 40¢ per serving.

Ingredients

1½ cups shredded Swiss cheese

½ cup grated Parmesan cheese

1½ teaspoons dried basil, crushed

2¾ cups water

1 cup yellow cornmeal

1 cup cold water

½ teaspoon salt

1 recipe Tomato-Basil Sauce (see below)

Tomato-Basil Sauce

In a medium saucepan stir together one 15-ounce can diced tomatoes with their juices, 2 tablespoons chopped fresh basil, and ½ teaspoon garlic salt. Simmer about 10 minutes or until reduced and thickened. Makes 1 cup sauce.

Directions

1 In a medium bowl stir together Swiss cheese, Parmesan cheese, and basil. Set aside. In a medium saucepan bring the 2¾ cups water to boiling.

2 Meanwhile, in another medium bowl stir together cornmeal, the 1 cup cold water, and the salt. See Photo A. Stir until combined.

3 Slowly add the cornmeal mixture to the boiling water, stirring constantly. See Photo B. Reduce heat to low and cook for 10 to 15 minutes or until mixture is very thick, stirring occasionally. See Photo C.

4 Pour one-third of the hot mixture into a greased 8x8-inch baking dish. Sprinkle with half of the cheese mixture. See Photo D. Repeat layers, ending with the hot mixture. Cool for 1 hour. Cover and chill several hours or overnight or until firm.

5 Preheat oven to 350°F. Bake polenta, uncovered, about 40 minutes or until lightly browned and heated through. Let stand for 10 minutes before serving. Serve with heated Tomato-Basil Sauce. *Serves 9.*

Nutrition Per Serving:

159 calories, 8g fat, 5g saturated fat, 2mg cholesterol, 285 mg sodium, 13g carbohydrate, 1g fiber, 9g protein

Swiss cheese, Parmesan cheese, and basil
make this updated version of Italian polenta
rich and inviting. Serve it plain or with Tomato-
Basil Sauce (see recipe, left) or your favorite
purchased gluten-free pasta sauce.

2

Special Health Benefits

Black-eyed peas have been a favorite of Southern cooks for more than 300 years. Not only do black-eyed peas taste great, they're also packed with good nutrition. Besides being high in protein, they are also a rich source of calcium, vitamin A, and folic acid. What's more, they're gluten-free.

Nutrition Per Serving:
265 calories, 3g fat, 1g saturated fat, 13mg cholesterol, 536 mg sodium, 45g carbohydrate, 7g fiber, 15g protein

Hoppin' John Ⓥ ⓛⓕ ⓔⓕ

Ingredients

1   15.8-ounce can black-eyed peas, drained, or 1 cup dried black-eyed peas
1   cup cold milk
1   tablespoon cornstarch
1   tablespoon butter
½   teaspoon salt
3   cups gluten-free chicken broth such as Better Than Bouillon®
1   tablespoon butter
1   cup white rice
½   cup diced cooked gluten-free ham (optional)
¼   cup chopped green sweet pepper
¼   cup finely chopped onion
Chopped sweet peppers (optional)

Directions

1 If using dried peas, soak peas overnight in a large bowl of cool water. See Photo A. When ready to cook, rinse and drain peas well.

2 Preheat oven to 350°F. For white sauce, in a small saucepan combine milk and cornstarch. Cook and stir until mixture boils; boil for 1 minute. Stir in 1 tablespoon butter and the salt. Remove from heat and set aside. (Note: For tips on making a simple gluten-free white sauce, see page 194.)

3 In a large saucepan combine peas, chicken broth, and 1 tablespoon butter; bring to a boil. If using canned peas, cook for 3 minutes; if using dried peas, cook for 15 minutes. Add rice to the broth mixture. See Photo B.

4 Cook just until the peas are tender. Use a fork to check for tenderness. See Photo C.

5 Shut off heat and stir in the white sauce, ham (if desired), the ¼ cup green pepper, and the onion. Pour into 2-quart casserole. Bake for about 40 minutes. If desired, garnish with additional chopped peppers. *Serves 6.*

Elizabeth says:
Using cornstarch instead of flour to make a white sauce gives recipes the same smooth texture and creamy flavor without the gluten.

A   B   C

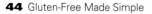

Folks in the Southern states say if you
have Hoppin' John on New Year's Day,
you'll have good luck all year long.

Wild Rice Casserole Ⓥ ⒺⒻ Ⓦⓖ

2

Special Health Benefits

Wild rice is not really a rice; it's a marsh grass. But like true rice, it does not contain gluten. Although low in fat, wild rice is high in protein, the amino acid lysine, and dietary fiber. It's also a good source of potassium and phosphorus and the B vitamins thiamin, riboflavin, and niacin. Look for it next to the regular rice at your local supermarket.

This mix of white and wild rices dressed up with mushrooms and pecans is the perfect partner for roast beef or pork, grilled chicken, or broiled fish.

Ingredients

1½ cups gluten-free chicken broth such as Better Than Bouillon®

2 tablespoons cornstarch

2 tablespoons butter

⅓ cup chopped celery

⅓ cup chopped onion

½ cup sliced mushrooms

1½ cups cooked wild rice

1½ cups cooked white rice

½ cup pecans

Directions

1 Preheat oven to 350°F. In a small saucepan stir together cool chicken broth and cornstarch until well mixed. Cook and stir over medium heat until mixture boils. Boil for 1 minute. Set aside.

2 In another small saucepan heat butter over medium-high heat. Add celery and onion and cook until soft. Add mushrooms and cook until tender.

3 In a large bowl mix cooked vegetables with the cooked wild rice and white rice. Add chicken broth mixture and stir to combine. Transfer to a greased 2-quart casserole and top with pecans. Cover and bake about 30 minutes or until bubbly. *Serves 8.*

Nutrition Per Serving:
164 calories, 9g fat, 3g saturated fat, 9mg cholesterol, 151 mg sodium, 19g carbohydrate, 2g fiber, 4g protein

Quinoa Tabbouleh Ⓥ ⒸⒻ ⒺⒻ ⓌⒼ

Ingredients

½ cup quinoa

1 cup gluten-free chicken broth such as Better Than Bouillon®

¾ cup chopped cucumber

½ cup snipped fresh parsley

¼ cup thinly sliced green onions

1 tablespoon snipped fresh mint

1 recipe Tabbouleh Dressing

¾ cup chopped tomato

4 lettuce leaves

Directions

1 Place quinoa in a colander and rinse with warm water for 2 minutes. **Note: quinoa must be rinsed VERY WELL to remove the bitterness on the grain.** In a saucepan, combine quinoa and chicken broth. Bring to a boil and let cook until quinoa splits and absorbs most of the chicken broth, about 15 minutes. Drain and cool.

2 In a large bowl combine quinoa, cucumber, parsley, green onions, and mint. Drizzle with Tabbouleh Dressing and toss to coat. Cover and chill for 4 to 24 hours. Stir tomato into quinoa mixture just before serving. Serve on lettuce leaves. *Serves 4.*

Tabbouleh Dressing: In a screw-top jar combine 3 tablespoons canola oil, 3 tablespoons lemon juice, 2 tablespoons water, and ¼ teaspoon salt. Cover and shake well.

Special Health Benefits
Quinoa contains a balanced set of essential amino acids making it an unusually complete protein source among plant foods. It is a good source of dietary fiber. It is also high in phosphorus, magnesium, and iron. And quinoa is naturally gluten-free and easy to digest.

Delightfully chewy and so very fresh, this quinoa version of tabbouleh will become a standard side dish to serve with grilled beef or fish.

Nutrition Per Serving:
188 calories, 12g fat, 2g saturated fat, 3mg cholesterol, 298 mg sodium, 16g carbohydrate, 2g fiber, 4g protein

Tofu with Veggies V CF EF

Read the Label

Purchased teriyaki sauce almost always contains wheat. But you can make a gluten-free version at home. Use the recipe at right and it's easy! Make extra and keep a supply in the refrigerator to use in other recipes that call for this sauce.

Special Health Benefits

Tofu is made from soybeans. Because of its unique amino acid content it is a good source of protein. It is also naturally gluten-ree.

Nutrition Per Serving:

174 calories, 11g fat, 2g saturated fat, 13mg cholesterol, 388 mg sodium, 13g carbohydrate, 2g fiber, 6g protein

Ingredients

- 1 12-ounce package extra-firm tofu, drained
- 1 recipe Gluten-Free Teriyaki Sauce
- ¼ cup cornmeal
- ⅛ teaspoon cayenne pepper
- 3 tablespoons olive oil
- ½ cup red sweet pepper strips
- ½ cup green sweet pepper strips
- ½ cup shredded carrots (optional)
- 1 cup snow pea pods, with strings and tips removed
- ½ cup sliced green onions or leeks

Gluten-Free Teriyaki Sauce

In a small bowl combine ¼ cup gluten-free soy sauce, 2 tablespoons honey, 2 tablespoons lemon juice, 1 teaspoon finely chopped onion, and ¼ teaspoon garlic powder. Mix and cover.

Directions

1 Cut tofu crosswise into eight slices. See Photo A. Arrange slices in a single layer in a baking dish. Set aside 2 tablespoons of the Gluten-Free Teriyaki Sauce. Pour the remaining teriyaki sauce over tofu, turning slices to coat. See Photo B. Let marinate at room temperature for 15 minutes.

2 Drain tofu, discarding marinade. In a shallow dish combine cornmeal and cayenne pepper. Carefully dip tofu slices in cornmeal mixture and press gently to coat both sides. Set tofu slices aside.

3 Pour 1 tablespoon of the olive oil into a large nonstick skillet. Add pepper strips and carrots (if desired); stir-fry over medium-high for 2 minutes. Add pea pods and green onions; stir-fry for 2 to 3 minutes more or until crisp-tender. See Photo C. Remove skillet from heat; stir in the reserved 2 tablespoons teriyaki sauce. Transfer vegetable mixture to a serving platter. Cover and keep warm. Wipe skillet clean.

4 In same skillet heat the remaining 2 tablespoons olive oil over medium heat. Add the coated tofu slices and cook for 2½ to 3 minutes on each side or until crisp and golden brown, using a fork or spatula to turn carefully. See Photo D. Serve tofu slices over vegetable mixture. *Serves 6.*

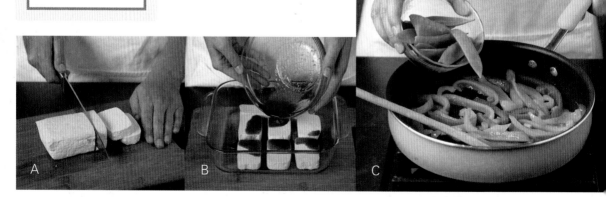

A   B   C

Golden crispy slices of cornmeal-coated tofu make this colorful stir-fry as hearty and satisfying as it is nutritious.

Asparagus Risotto Ⓥ Ⓔ🅕

2

Where to Find It

Arborio rice is an Italian short-grain rice with a higher amount of soluble starch that's released during cooking. Naturally gluten-free, Arborio rice is the ideal choice for risotto because it gives the dish a creamy consistency. It's also great for soups and rice puddings. Look for it with the other rices in large supermarkets or health-food stores.

Ingredients

½ pound asparagus, trimmed and cut into 2-inch pieces

2½ cups gluten-free chicken broth such as Better Than Bouillon®

2 tablespoons olive oil

¼ cup finely chopped onion

¾ cup Arborio rice

¼ cup water

¼ cup freshly grated Parmesan cheese

2 tablespoons butter

Shaved Parmesan cheese (optional)

Directions

1 In a small saucepan cook asparagus in boiling water for 2 minutes; drain and rinse with cold water. Set aside. In same small saucepan heat chicken broth on low heat.

2 In a heavy, large saucepan heat olive oil over medium heat. Add onion and cook about 4 minutes or until tender. Add rice and cook for 3 minutes, stirring constantly. See Photo A. Add the ¼ cup water and cook about 1 minute or until evaporated. See Photo B.

3 Add ½ cup of the hot broth and stir constantly. See Photo C. When most of the liquid is absorbed by the rice (about 3 minutes), add another ½ cup of the broth and stir constantly until most of the liquid is absorbed. See Photo D. Repeat stirring and adding broth ½ cup at a time until all broth is incorporated and rice is tender but still slightly firm in center and mixture is creamy (about 20 minutes total). Add asparagus and cook for 2 minutes. Remove from heat. Stir in the grated Parmesan cheese and butter. Serve immediately. If desired, sprinkle with shaved Parmesan cheese. *Serves 6.*

Nutrition Per Serving:

194 calories, 10g fat, 4g saturated fat, 14mg cholesterol, 296 mg sodium, 22g carbohydrate, 1g fiber, 5g protein

Sweet Potato Fries Ⓥ ⓁⒻ ⒸⒻ ⒺⒻ

Special Health Benefits

The sweet potato is a nutrition powerhouse. One large sweet potato furnishes almost twice the recommended daily allowance of vitamin A, 42% of vitamin C, and four times the beta carotene. When you eat a sweet potato with the skin on, it has more fiber than oatmeal. And sweet potatoes are naturally gluten-free.

Add a Flavor Variation

If you have a favorite fresh herb, such as basil or dill, try it in this easy-to-make recipe instead of the rosemary.

Nutrition Per Serving:

86 calories, 3g fat, 0g saturated fat, 0mg cholesterol, 617mg sodium, 13g carbohydrate, 2g fiber, 1g protein

Ingredients

2 large sweet potatoes
3 tablespoons olive oil
2 stalks fresh rosemary
1 teaspoon coarse sea salt
1 teaspoon pepper

Directions

1 Preheat oven to 400°F. Peel the sweet potatoes and cut into ½-inch-wide strips. Set aside.

2 Pour the olive oil into a shallow baking pan. Remove the leaves from the rosemary and scatter over the oil. See Photo A.

3 Spread the sweet potatoes on the baking pan. See Photo B. With a spatula, turn the potatoes so they are coated with oil on both sides. See Photo C.

4 Sprinkle potatoes with sea salt and pepper. Bake about 10 minutes. With spatula, turn potatoes and bake about 5 minutes longer or until potatoes are crisp-tender. Serve immediately. *Serves 4.*

Marcia says:

Our children love these fries—but they prefer them made without any herbs. To keep everyone happy, we make two pans—one for the adults and one for the kids!

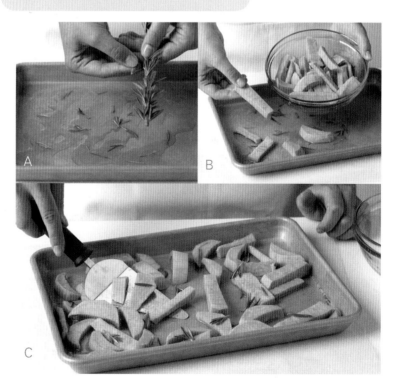

A

B

C

When you're serving burgers, bake up
a batch of these pretty sweet potatoes,
too. You'll love the combination!

Grains and Side Dishes

2

Plan Ahead and Save Time

Crush a boxful of Corn Chex® all at once and store the crumbs in a canister to have on hand for recipes that call for them.

Add a Flavor Variation

Try adding ½ cup chopped gluten-free ham to this creamy corn. Because ham is high in sodium, decrease the salt to ½ teaspoon.

Nutrition Per Serving:

141 calories, 8g fat, 4g saturated fat, 95mg cholesterol, 356 mg sodium, 14g carbohydrate, 1g fiber, 5g protein

Scalloped Corn **V** **LF** **WG**

Ingredients

Butter

2 cups Corn Chex®

3 eggs

¾ cup milk

2 tablespoons chopped red sweet pepper

¼ cup butter, melted

1 teaspoon salt

½ teaspoon black pepper

3 cups frozen or fresh whole kernel corn

4 tablespoons gluten-free bread crumbs such as Kinnikinnick® Panko-style Bread Crumbs, (optional)

Directions

1 Preheat oven to 350°F. Grease a 1½-quart baking dish or casserole with butter. Set aside.

2 Place Corn Chex® in a plastic bag and crush with a rolling pin. See Photo A. Measure ¾ cup crushed cereal; set aside. Save any remaining crushed cereal for another use.

3 Beat eggs and milk until well mixed. Add sweet pepper, the ¼ cup melted butter, the salt, black pepper, and crushed Corn Chex® and mix well. See Photo B.

4 Add corn. See Photo C. Mix well and pour into baking dish. If desired, top with buttered gluten-free bread crumbs. Bake for 45 minutes. *Serves 8.*

Carol says:

The crushed Corn Chex® cereal in this recipe replaces the usual crackers in traditional scalloped corn. The crumbs soften up just like crackers, making the corn mixture rich and creamy.

A

B

C

You'll have no trouble getting the family to eat vegetables with this appealing casserole. Corn, sweet pepper, Corn Chex® cereal, and butter guarantee the flavor is top-notch. Be sure to make enough so everyone can have seconds.

By law, in the United States wheat products are enriched and fortified with B vitamins, folate, and iron. This law was passed years ago to decrease nutritional deficiencies, which were very common at the time. However, with the exception of white rice, other flours and starches are not enriched with vitamins and minerals. Thus, people on a gluten-free diet are often missing out on these essential nutrients. In addition, the refined starches that are frequently used in a gluten-free diet are low in fiber and nutrients. It is very important that individuals eating gluten-free choose whole-grain foods whenever possible to increase the amount of nutrients in their diets.

Elizabeth says:
When choosing and developing the recipes in this book we have tried to include a number of recipes with whole grains. Look for the icon at the top of each recipe page to see if the recipe contains a whole grain.

- Choose brown rice instead of white rice. Brown rice has much more fiber and is a great source of B vitamins.

- Try to consume at least 3 servings of whole grains per day, such as quinoa, brown rice, and corn.

- Teff flour, amaranth flour, quinoa flour, buckwheat flour, cornmeal, corn flour, and brown rice flour are all whole-grain foods.

- Add whole grains such as cooked quinoa to salads or casseroles. They add texture as well as nutritional value.

3 Salads, Fruits, and Vegetables

Greek Salad Ⓥ ⒺⒻ

The Cost

Making your own dressing saves money and guarantees the dressing is gluten-free. The cost for the dressing recipe is about $1.25.

Where to Find It

Feta cheese is a staple of Greek cooking. In this salad it adds a zesty tang. Look for it in the specialty cheese section at large grocery stores.

Nutrition Per Serving:
276 calories, 25g fat, 3g saturated fat, 7mg cholesterol, 185mg sodium, 12g carbohydrate, 4g fiber, 3g protein.

Ingredients

3½ pounds romaine lettuce, washed and torn into bite-size pieces

6 Roma tomatoes, diced

2 cucumbers, peeled and sliced

¾ cup whole black olives

½ of a medium red onion, sliced into rings

½ cup feta cheese crumbles

1 recipe Greek Vinaigrette Dressing (see recipe, right)

Feta cheese crumbles (optional)

Directions

1 Place lettuce in a large bowl. Add tomatoes, cucumbers, olives, onion, and the ½ cup feta cheese. Toss lightly to mix all ingredients. Add Greek Vinaigrette Dressing and toss to serve. If desired, top with more feta cheese. *Serves 10.*

Greek Vinaigrette Dressing: Mince 1 clove of garlic by first removing skin on garlic. Then lay the flat side of a wide knife on the garlic clove and use your fist to smash the clove. See Photo A. Set aside. In a medium bowl combine the garlic, ¾ cup gluten-free red wine vinegar, ⅓ cup water, 2 tablespoons sugar, 2 tablespoons dried basil, 2 tablespoons dried oregano, and 2 tablespoons Dijon-style gluten-free mustard. Mix well. See Photo B. Gradually pour in 1 cup canola oil while beating with a wire whisk. See Photo C. Refrigerate until ready to serve. *Serves 10.*

Marcia says:

For a unique gift for a friend who's also on a gluten-free diet, I filled a pretty bottle with this dressing and attached a copy of the recipe.

A

B

C

This delightful medley of romaine lettuce, Roma tomatoes, olives, cucumbers, and feta cheese is topped with a tangy gluten-free dressing seasoned with basil, oregano, and Dijon–style mustard.

Broccoli-Cheese Salad Ⓥ

**Special
Health Benefits**
*Broccoli is a plant
from the kale family.
It is high in calcium,
an essential mineral
for bone and muscle
function. It is also
high in vitamins C,
K, and A, as well as
dietary fiber.*

3

Ingredients

1 14-ounce package
broccoli slaw or 3 cups
chopped broccoli,
¾ cup shredded
cabbage, and ½ cup
shredded carrots

1 cup cubed Colby-Jack
cheese

½ cup crumbled cooked
bacon

½ cup gluten-free
mayonnaise such
as Hellmann's/
Best Foods® Real
Mayonnaise

¼ cup lemon juice

½ teaspoon salt

¼ teaspoon pepper

Directions

1 In a large bowl combine slaw mixture, cubed
cheese, and bacon. Set aside.

2 In a small bowl mix mayonnaise, lemon juice, salt,
and pepper until well mixed. Pour mayonnaise
mixture over slaw mixture and toss to combine.
Serve immediately or refrigerate for up to 2 hours.
Serves 6.

The crunchiness
of the shredded
broccoli and the
soft cheese cubes
combine to make
an enticing and tasty
quick-to-fix salad.

**Nutrition
Per Serving:**
129 calories, 9g
fat, 5g saturated
fat, 25mg
cholesterol,
300mg sodium, 5g
carbohydrate, 1g
fiber, 8g protein

Glazed Pears (V) (EF)

Ingredients

2 large fresh pears
3 tablespoons water
1 tablespoon lemon juice
¼ cup butter
⅓ cup packed brown sugar
¼ cup dried cranberries
¼ cup sliced almonds

Directions

1 Wash the pears and cut into ½-inch slices. In a small bowl mix the water and lemon juice. Place the pears in the lemon juice mixture. Set aside.

2 In a medium skillet melt butter on medium-high heat. Remove pears from liquid and pat dry. Add pear slices to butter and cook about 2 minutes or just until starting to brown, turning to cook evenly. Add the brown sugar and cranberries. Reduce heat and cook about 1 minute or until mixture thickens slightly. Serve immediately. Sprinkle with sliced almonds. *Serves 4.*

Carol says:
The brown sugar and butter form a thick, sweet glaze for the pears so no additional thickening is needed.

Add a Flavor Variation
If your family likes golden raisins or dried currants, use them in place of the cranberries. You can also switch apples for the pears. However, they will take a few more minutes to cook.

The Cost
Pears are available almost year round at reasonable prices. Each pear will serve two people a luscious, yet inexpensive treat.

This delightful dessert boasts red pears and dried cranberries lightly glazed with a brown sugar mixture and topped with sliced almonds.

Nutrition Per Serving:
275 calories, 16g fat, 8g saturated fat, 31mg cholesterol, 9mg sodium, 33g carbohydrate, 4g fiber, 2g protein

Easy Cabbage Salad Ⓥ ⓁⒻ ⒸⒻ ⒺⒻ

3

Read the Label

Most high-quality canned fruits and vegetables are gluten-free. However, always read the label and avoid products that have words like "caramel coloring" or "artificial flavors" on the label.

Special Health Benefits

Cabbage is high in vitamin K, an essential vitamin for blood and bone health. Almonds contain vitamin E, a powerful antioxidant.

Zesty gluten-free Italian salad dressing gives this fresh-tasting cabbage and orange combination irresistible flavor.

Ingredients

1 14-ounce package shredded cabbage with carrots or 4 cups shredded cabbage

1 10-ounce can mandarin oranges, drained

¼ cup whole almonds

½ cup gluten-free Italian dressing such as Newman's Own® Oil and Vinegar Salad Dressing

Directions

1 In a large bowl combine the cabbage, oranges, and almonds. Add the dressing and toss to mix thoroughly. Serve immediately or chill for up to 2 hours. *Serves 8.*

Marcia says:
This salad is easy to make because it uses pre-packaged cabbage slaw. I can have it ready to serve in under 10 minutes.

Nutrition Per Serving:

120 calories, 8g fat, 1g saturated fat, 10mg cholesterol, 20mg sodium, 9g carbohydrate, 2g fiber, 3g protein

Best Egg Salad Ⓥ

Ingredients

6 hard-cooked eggs, cooled and chopped

¼ cup shredded zucchini

¼ cup shredded carrot

¼ cup chopped celery

1 tablespoon chopped green onion

¼ cup cream cheese, softened

2 tablespoons gluten-free mayonnaise such as Hellmann's/ Best Foods® Real Mayonnaise

¼ teaspoon dried dillweed

Dash *each* dry mustard, salt, and pepper

Directions

1 For tips on hard-cooking eggs, see page 192.

2 In a large bowl combine chopped eggs, zucchini, carrot, celery, and green onion. In a small bowl stir together cream cheese, mayonnaise, and the seasonings until well mixed. Stir cream cheese mixture into egg mixture. Cover and refrigerate until cool. Serve on a lettuce leaf with gluten-free crackers. *Serves 6.*

Elizabeth says:
Eggs contain the highest quality protein of any food. They also contain choline, an essential nutrient for brain function.

Plan Ahead and Save Time
Cook and refrigerate the eggs the day before you plan to make the egg salad. The cold eggs will be easier to peel. Cooked eggs will keep in the refrigerator for up to a week according to the American Egg Board.

For a main dish, serve this egg salad on a lettuce leaf. To tote it to work, create a great sandwich with Feta-Basil Bread (see recipe, page 82).

Nutrition Per Serving:
147 calories, 12g fat, 4g saturated fat, 225mg cholesterol, 150mg sodium, 2g carbohydrate, 0g fiber, 7g protein

Broiled Tomatoes ⓥ

Read the Label

Be sure to read the label or check with the manufacturer when choosing any dressing product such as mayonnaise. Beware of words like "food starch", or "emulsifiers" in the ingredients list. These general terms may mean there is gluten in the product. See page188 for more about reading labels.

Ingredients

- 2 medium to large tomatoes
- ⅓ cup gluten-free mayonnaise such as Hellmann's/ Best Foods® Real Mayonnaise
- ⅓ cup gluten-free plain yogurt or dairy sour cream
- ½ teaspoon salt
- ½ teaspoon pepper
- 4 tablespoons shredded Parmesan cheese
- 4 sprigs fresh basil

Directions

1 Preheat oven to 400°F. Wash and remove stems from tomatoes. Carefully halve the tomatoes crosswise, keeping the cuts as level as possible. See Photo A. Place on a baking sheet. Set aside.

2 In a small bowl mix together the mayonnaise, yogurt, salt, and pepper. Carefully spread the mixture over the tomatoes. See Photo B.

3 Sprinkle tomatoes with Parmesan cheese and top each with a basil sprig. See Photo C. Bake for 10 minutes. Turn oven to broil and broil about 1 minute or until cheese is bubbly and brown. (*Note:* Watch tomatoes carefully because the cheese can burn quickly.) *Serves 4.*

Carol says:
Whether you're using yogurt or sour cream in this recipe, you'll get a great tangy flavor that complements the fresh tomato.

Nutrition Per Serving:
185 calories, 16g fat, 3g saturated fat, 17mg cholesterol, 412mg sodium, 6g carbohydrate, 1g fiber, 5g protein

A

B

C

The creamy mayonnaise, yogurt, and Parmesan cheese topper brings out the best in ripe, summer-fresh tomatoes. For a colorful presentation, use a mix of red, yellow, and orange tomato halves.

Fruit Pasta Salad 🅥 🅒🅕 🅔🅕

Special Health Benefits

Cantaloupe, peaches, strawberries, and kiwifruit are all high in vitamin C, an essential vitamin that boosts the immune system.

Add a Flavor Variation

For a change of pace, try sliced banana or pear instead of the sliced peaches.

3

Twisted corn pasta is an eye-catching shape for this fresh fruit pasta salad, but other gluten-free pastas such as bow-ties and elbow macaroni are attractive, too.

Nutrition Per Serving:
201 calories, 13g fat, 1g saturated fat, 0mg cholesterol, 10mg sodium, 22g carbohydrate, 3g fiber, 2g protein

Ingredients

1½ cups gluten-free small pasta shapes

½ cup cubed cantaloupe

½ cup cut-up peeled fresh peaches

½ cup sliced fresh strawberries

½ cup sliced, peeled kiwifruit

½ cup finely chopped celery

1 recipe Lemon-Poppy Seed Dressing (see recipe, right)

Directions

1 Cook pasta following directions on package. Rinse and drain. Set aside.

2 In a large bowl combine cantaloupe, peaches, strawberries, and kiwifruit. Add cooked pasta and celery and mix well. Add Lemon-Poppy Seed Dressing and toss to coat. Chill for 6 hours or overnight. *Serves 6.*

Lemon-Poppy Seed Dressing: In a food processor or blender combine 3 tablespoons sugar, 1 teaspoon grated lemon peel, 2 tablespoons lemon juice, 1 tablespoon finely chopped green onion, and ¼ teaspoon pepper. Cover and blend until combined.

With blender running, slowly add ⅓ cup canola oil through the hole in lid, blending until mixture is slightly thickened. Stir in 1 teaspoon poppy seeds. Serve immediately or cover and store in refrigerator for up to a week. Shake well before serving.

Radish Salad Ⓥ

Ingredients

1 cup gluten-free dairy sour cream

3 tablespoons gluten-free mayonnaise such as Hellmann's/Best Foods® Real Mayonnaise

1 teaspoon finely chopped onion

1 small clove garlic, crushed

¼ teaspoon salt

¼ teaspoon black pepper

1 cup drained, cooked or canned garbanzo beans

6 cups bite-size lettuce pieces

½ cup sliced radishes

½ cup sliced, pitted gluten-free ripe olives

⅓ cup chopped green sweet pepper

Directions

1 In a medium bowl combine sour cream, mayonnaise, onion, garlic, salt, and black pepper. Stir in garbanzo beans. Chill for at least 1 hour.

2 In a large bowl combine lettuce, radishes, olives, and green pepper. Add chilled garbanzo bean mixture and mix well. Serve immediately. *Serves 8.*

Elizabeth says:
Garbanzo beans are a great source of fiber and protein, have a long shelf life, and are inexpensive.

Plan Ahead and Save Time
The garbanzo bean-and-sour cream mixture can be made ahead—even the day before. Just be sure to keep it covered in the refrigerator until you're ready to add it to the lettuce mixture.

Garbanzo beans, radishes, green pepper, and gluten-free olives team up to make this creamy tossed salad sensational. Serve it with grilled or broiled chicken or pork chops.

Nutrition Per Serving:
172 calories, 13g fat, 6g saturated fat, 25mg cholesterol, 312mg sodium, 10g carbohydrate, 2g fiber, 4g protein

Tomato Aspic **V** **LF** **CF**

3

Read the Label

Most gelatins, such as Jell-O® Gelatin, are gluten-free. Olives are also an ingredient to check before using because some have gluten and others do not. Hot sauce or red pepper sauce can also be a problem. Tabasco® brand is gluten-free. If the product is not clearly labeled "gluten-free," then carefully read the label or call the manufacturer.

Ingredients

1 3-ounce package gluten-free lemon-flavor gelatin such as Jell-O®

1¼ cups boiling water

1 5½-ounce can gluten-free vegetable juice such as V8®

1½ tablespoons gluten-free vinegar

½ teaspoon salt

⅛ teaspoon gluten-free hot pepper sauce such as Tabasco®

Dash ground cloves

3 large stalks celery

¼ cup sliced gluten-free green or black olives

¼ cup shredded carrot

¼ cup gluten-free mayonnaise such as Hellmann's/Best Foods® Real Mayonnaise

1 teaspoon chopped fresh chives

Directions

1 Place gelatin in large bowl and pour the boiling water over gelatin. Stir until gelatin is dissolved. Stir in vegetable juice, vinegar, salt, hot pepper sauce, and cloves. See Photo A.

2 Chill about 15 minutes or until thick but not set. Meanwhile, dice celery stalks. Lay trimmed stalks on cutting board and use a sharp knife to cut each stalk into 4 long lengthwise pieces. Then chop the stalks as evenly as possible. See Photo B.

3 When the gelatin is thick, remove from refrigerator and fold in the celery, olives, and carrot. See Photo C.

4 Pour mixture into molds such as 6-ounce custard cups. See Photo D. Refrigerate until set. In a small bowl mix mayonnaise and chives. Remove gelatin from molds and top with mayonnaise mixture. *Serves 6.*

A

B

C

D

Nutrition Per Serving:
139 calories, 8g fat, 1g saturated fat, 5mg cholesterol, 391 mg sodium, 16g carbohydrate, 1g fiber, 2g protein

Tomato aspic is a vintage salad that's been popular
for generations. This version uses lemon gelatin and
vegetable juice instead of the traditional unflavored gelatin
and tomato juice. Its seasonings and flavors are just right
for today's modern tastes.

Classic Chicken Salad 🅷🅿 🅒🅕

3

Add a Flavor Variation

If you prefer walnuts instead of almonds, substitute ¼ cup of chopped walnuts in place of the almonds. Then, to add a whole grain, sprinkle with cooked quinoa.

Grapes, carrot, and almonds make this creamy classic, made with chunks of tender chicken breast, extra tasty.

Nutrition Per Serving:
384 calories, 25g fat, 4g saturated fat, 101mg cholesterol, 321 mg sodium, 5g carbohydrate, 1g fiber, 35g protein

Ingredients

3   cups water
1   stalk celery
1   carrot, diced
1   tablespoon bouillon such as Better Than Bouillon®
1   teaspoon salt
3   skinless, boneless chicken breast halves
½   cup chopped celery
1   tablespoon thinly sliced green onion
½   cup gluten-free mayonnaise such as Hellmann's/Best Foods® Real Mayonnaise
1   tablespoon lemon juice
½   cup sliced green grapes
¼   cup whole almonds
Romaine lettuce leaves

Directions

1 In a small saucepan bring the water, celery stalk, carrot, bouillon, and salt to boiling. Cut chicken breasts into 2-inch pieces and place in boiling water. Cover and cook about 15 minutes or until chicken is tender and fully cooked. Remove from liquid and cool. Refrigerate until ready to use.

2 Cut the cooled chicken into 1-inch pieces. In a large bowl combine chicken, chopped celery, and green onion. Stir together mayonnaise and lemon juice and stir into chicken mixture. Keep refrigerated until ready to serve. Add the grapes and almonds just before serving. Serve on romaine lettuce leaves. *Serves 5.*

Apple-Walnut Salad Ⓥ ⒠

Ingredients

1 large Granny Smith apple

Juice of 1 small lemon

4 cups bite-size romaine lettuce pieces

½ cup golden raisins

½ cup chopped walnuts

¼ cup gluten-free blue cheese crumbles

2 tablespoons sliced green onion

1 recipe Sweet Honey Dressing (see recipe, right)

Dried apple slices

Directions

1 Wash and cut Granny Smith apple into small pieces and place in a small bowl. Add lemon juice and toss. Set aside.

2 In a large bowl mix the lettuce, raisins, walnuts, blue cheese crumbles, and green onion. Add the Granny Smith apple pieces and mix well. Toss with the Sweet Honey Dressing until coated. Garnish with dried apple slices. Serve immediately. *Serves 6.*

Sweet Honey Dressing: In a jar with a lid combine ⅓ cup salad oil, ⅓ cup gluten-free wine vinegar, 1 tablespoon chopped fresh basil, 1 tablespoon honey, ¼ teaspoon dry mustard, and ⅛ teaspoon pepper. Shake dressing and pour over the salad.

Special Health Benefits

Apples are high in fiber and are full of antioxidants, while walnuts are a great source of omega-3 fatty acids, which some studies indicate may help lower cholesterol.

Tart Granny Smith apples and tangy blue cheese are the perfect counterpoints to the sweet raisins and Sweet Honey Dressing of this salad. The walnuts add a delightful flavor and crunch.

Nutrition Per Serving: 240 calories, 20g fat, 3g saturated fat, 4 mg cholesterol, 89 mg sodium, 13g carbohydrate, 4g fiber, 4g protein

Salads, Fruits, and Vegetables

Read the Label

While natural cheeses are gluten-free, processed cheeses, including some blue cheeses, may have gluten. Always read the label or contact the manufacturer when in doubt.

3

Blue Cheese Veggies **V** **LF** **EF**

Ingredients

1 large seedless cucumber

2 small Roma tomatoes

Gluten-free blue cheese dressing

Gluten-free blue cheese crumbles

1 tablespoon chopped fresh dill or 2 teaspoons dried dill weed

Salt and pepper

Fresh dill sprig

Directions

1 Wash and partially peel the cucumber. Cut into thin slices. Set aside.

2 Wash but do not peel the tomatoes. Cut into thin slices. Arrange the cucumber and tomatoes on 4 plates. Drizzle blue cheese dressing over the vegetable combination.

3 Sprinkle with blue cheese crumbles. Sprinkle with chopped dill, salt, and pepper. If desired, garnish with dill sprig. *Serves 4.*

If you have your own garden or love to go to farmers' markets, remember this simple, yet full-flavored recipe when the new crop of tomatoes and cucumbers is at its peak.

Nutrition Per Serving:
59 calories, 4g fat, 1g saturated fat, 5mg cholesterol, 114mg sodium, 4g carbohydrate, 1g fiber, 2g protein

Waldorf Salad Ⓥ

Ingredients

2 cups coarsely chopped crisp apples such as Granny Smith or Gala

Juice of 1 small lemon

1 cup chopped celery

½ cup chopped walnuts

½ cup sliced green grapes

¼ cup dried cranberries

½ cup gluten-free mayonnaise such as Hellmann's/ Best Foods® Real Mayonnaise

¼ cup gluten-free plain yogurt

2 tablespoons lemon juice

Directions

1 Place apples in a small bowl. Add the juice from small lemon and toss to coat.

2 In a large bowl combine celery, walnuts, grapes, and dried cranberries. Add the apple and mix well. Stir together the mayonnaise, yogurt, and the 2 tablespoons lemon juice; add to apple mixture and toss to coat. *Serves 4.*

Add a Flavor Variation

Create your own take on old-fashioned Waldorf Salad by replacing the apples with fresh pears, the cranberries with dried cherries, and the walnuts with pecans.

The first Waldorf Salad was served at the Waldorf-Astoria Hotel in the late 1800s. At first, it only had apples, celery, and mayonnaise, but later the walnuts became a standard ingredient.

Nutrition Per Serving: 370 calories, 32g fat, 4g saturated fat, 17mg cholesterol, 41 mg sodium, 22g carbohydrate, 3g fiber, 4g protein

Stir-Fried Kale EF

Special Health Benefits

Kale is an excellent source of vitamin K, an essential vitamin for blood and bone health. The current nutritional guidelines recommend that everyone consume a variety of colors of vegetables every day. This salad lets you enjoy dark green, light green, and orange vegetables all at once.

The chicken strips make this warm green salad a satisfying main dish. If you're looking for a lively side dish, serve it without the chicken.

Ingredients

1   skinless, boneless chicken breast half
2   tablespoons canola oil
½   cup chopped celery
¼   cup sliced green onion
1   tablespoon butter
2   tablespoons olive oil
½   cup bite-size green bean pieces
½   cup shredded carrot
2   cups chopped fresh kale
½   cup broccoli flowerets
¼   cup gluten-free white wine
½   teaspoon salt
½   teaspoon pepper

Directions

1 Cut chicken into long thin strips. In a small skillet heat the canola oil on medium heat. Add chicken strips and cook until tender and no longer pink. Remove from skillet and place in small bowl. Cover to keep warm.

2 In the same skillet heat butter and cook celery and green onion. Add the olive oil. Add green beans and carrot and cook for 1 minute. Add kale and broccoli and cook about 1 minute longer or until tender. Add white wine, salt, and pepper and heat through.

3 Top vegetables with chicken strips. Serve immediately. *Serves 4.*

Nutrition Per Serving:
180 calories, 12g fat, 3g saturated fat, 25 mg cholesterol, 350mg sodium, 8g carbohydrate, 2g fiber, 9g protein

Tuna Salad **HP** **CF**

Ingredients

2 6-ounce cans white albacore tuna, drained

¼ cup chopped celery

1 teaspoon finely chopped green onion or fresh chives

½ teaspoon salt

¼ teaspoon pepper

¼ teaspoon dried dill weed

½ cup gluten-free mayonnaise such as Hellmann's/Best Foods® Real Mayonnaise

½ cup chopped cucumber

Directions

1 In a medium bowl mix tuna, celery, and green onion. Add salt, pepper, and dill weed and mix well. Add mayonnaise and toss lightly.

2 Gently stir in cucumber just before serving. Serve on lettuce leaves or on gluten-free bread. *Serves 6.*

Marcia says:

This is a salad that I make often for a quick lunch or dinner. I usually serve it on a slice of Feta-Basil Bread (see recipe, page 82).

Read the Label
Almost all canned meats and fish are gluten-free. However, processed meats and meat products such as frankfurters, ham, and pepperoni may contain gluten. Read the label carefully before selecting a brand.

Albacore tuna has the lightest flesh and mildest flavor of all tunas. Here it's combined with dill weed and cucumber in a can't miss salad that tastes terrific.

Nutrition Per Serving:
207 calories, 16g fat, 3g saturated fat, 35mg cholesterol, 231 mg sodium, 1g carbohydrate, 0g fiber, 14g protein

Fruits and vegetables are a vital part of every person's diet, regardless of age, gender, or health. Fruits and vegetables provide essential nutrients and fiber and may play a role in preventing many chronic diseases. Studies have indicated that eating more fruits and vegetables may decrease the risk of stroke, Type 2 diabetes, some types of cancer, as well as cardiovascular disease and hypertension.

It is important to eat several different colors of fruits and vegetables each week because each color correlates with certain vitamins and minerals. For instance, orange indicates large amounts of vitamin A, while dark green indicates large amounts of calcium and vitamin K.

Elizabeth says:
The exact recommendations for fruits and vegetables to be consumed each day varies from person to person, but overall individuals should consume 2 to 4 cups of fruit and 3 to 4 cups of vegetables.

Try these tips to increase your daily fruit and vegetable intake while staying on a gluten-free diet:

- Start the day with a glass of 100% juice with breakfast.

- Make a fresh fruit bowl with oranges, grapefruits, apples, and bananas. Place the bowl on the kitchen table or in a location that you look at frequently. Seeing the fruit will remind you to eat it more often.

- Serve tortilla chips and salsa as a snack; salsa contains tomatoes and peppers, both great sources of vitamin C. Each ½ cup of salsa counts as a ½ cup toward meeting your daily vegetable needs.

- For an easy, nutritious dinner, serve baked potatoes stuffed with broccoli, chopped tomatoes, shredded carrots, and cheese.

- Always have fresh vegetables cleaned and ready in the refrigerator for snacking.

4 Breads and Muffins

Blueberry-Orange Scones Ⓥ ⒺⒻ

Add a Flavor Variation

Substitute dried cranberries or dried currants for the blueberries. Or add chopped walnuts, almonds, or pecans.

Freeze for Later:

These scones can be made and frozen in freezer containers for up to 6 months. Add the drizzle just before serving.

Nutrition Per Serving:

277 calories, 12g fat, 7g saturated fat, 31mg cholesterol, 324 mg sodium, 40g carbohydrate, 2g fiber, 3g protein

Recipe courtesy of Domata Living™

Ingredients

- 2 cups Domata Living™ gluten-free all-purpose flour
- 2 tablespoons sugar
- 1 tablespoon baking powder
- ½ teaspoon baking soda
- ¼ teaspoon salt
- 1 tablespoon grated orange peel
- ½ cup very cold, unsalted butter, cut up
- 1 cup dried blueberries
- ⅔ cup buttermilk
- 1 recipe Orange Frosting Drizzle

Directions

1 Preheat oven to 425°F. Lightly grease a baking sheet. Set aside. In a large bowl combine flour, sugar, baking powder, baking soda, and salt. Add grated orange peel and mix well. See Photo A.

2 Using a pastry blender, cut in butter until mixture is crumbly, resembling small peas. See Photo B. Add dried blueberries and buttermilk, stirring until just moistened. Turn dough out onto a lightly floured surface; knead 5 or 6 times. See Photo C.

3 Pat into an 8-inch circle. Cut into 8 wedges. See Photo D. Place 1 inch apart on prepared baking sheet. Bake about 15 minutes or until golden brown. Let cool. Drizzle with Orange Frosting Drizzle. *Serves 8.*

Orange Frosting Drizzle: In a small bowl stir together 2 cups powdered sugar, 2 tablespoons orange juice, 1 tablespoon melted butter, and 1 teaspoon grated orange peel until creamy and smooth. Place in a piping tube or a small plastic sandwich bag; cut off corner of bag. Pipe or squeeze frosting onto scones.
Note: For tips on drizzling baked items, see page 194.

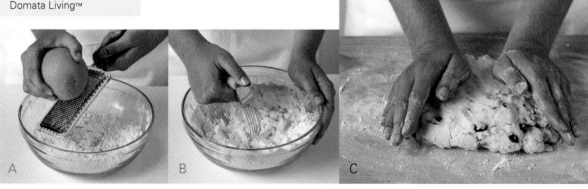

A   B   C

Pleasingly dense and not crumbly in texture, these scones have so much blueberry and orange flavor there's no need to serve them with butter or jam.

Pineapple Muffins Ⓥ ⓁⒻ ⒸⒻ

Plan Ahead and Save Time

Make this muffin batter and keep it in the refrigerator for up to 24 hours so you can bake the muffins right before serving. Then freeze the leftovers so you'll have a supply on hand to take out a few at a time, whenever you need them.

Shredded carrot, crushed pineapple, and raisins make these tender muffins slightly sweet. They're just the ticket for brunch or afternoon tea.

Ingredients

2 cups gluten-free all-purpose flour such as Bob's Red Mill®

½ cup sugar

2 teaspoons baking powder

½ teaspoon ground cinnamon

¼ teaspoon ground ginger

2 eggs, beaten

1 8-ounce can crushed pineapple, undrained

½ cup shredded carrot

½ cup golden raisins

¼ cup canola oil

1 teaspoon vanilla

½ cup chopped pecans (optional)

1 recipe Powdered Sugar Drizzle (see page 124) (optional)

Directions

1 Preheat oven to 375°F. Grease 24 muffin cups. Set aside. In a large bowl combine flour, sugar, baking powder, cinnamon, and ginger.

2 In a medium bowl mix eggs, pineapple with juice, carrot, raisins, oil, and vanilla. Slowly pour egg mixture into dry ingredients and stir until just moistened. If desired, fold in nuts.

3 Fill prepared muffins cups three-fourths full. Bake about 20 minutes or until golden brown. Cool for 3 minutes before removing from cups. If desired, drizzle with Powdered Sugar Icing. Keep muffins refrigerated after baking. *Serves 24.*

Note: For tips on drizzling icing, see page 194.

Nutrition Per Serving:
107 calories, 3g fat, 0g saturated fat, 18 mg cholesterol, 51 mg sodium, 20g carbohydrate, 1g fiber, 2g protein

Buttery Corn Bread **V** **WG**

Ingredients

1½ cups cornmeal

¾ cup brown rice flour

½ cup tapioca flour

½ cup sugar

1 tablespoon baking powder

1 teaspoon salt

3 eggs

¾ cup buttermilk

⅓ cup canola oil

2 tablespoons carbonated water

Directions

1 Preheat oven to 375°F. Grease an 8x8-inch baking pan. Set aside. In a large mixing bowl combine cornmeal, rice flour, tapioca flour, sugar, baking powder, and salt. Make a well in the center of the dry ingredients.

2 In a medium bowl mix eggs, buttermilk, oil, and carbonated water. Pour into dry ingredients and mix well. Batter will be thin. Pour into prepared pan.

3 Bake for 15 minutes. Reduce heat to 350°F. Bake about 10 minutes more or until a wooden toothpick comes out clean inserted in the center. *Serves 9.*

Where to Find It

Rice flour and tapioca flour are available at most large grocery stores and health food stores. One easy-to-find brand is Bob's Red Mill®.

This fine-textured corn bread has appealing color and a remarkably rich flavor. Serve it with honey butter or raspberry jam.

Nutrition Per Serving:
257 calories, 11g fat, 1g saturated fat, 71mg cholesterol, 475 mg sodium, 35g carbohydrate, 3g fiber, 6g protein

Freeze for Later

Make a double batch of this savory bread so you'll have plenty on hand. Slice each loaf, seal it in a freezer bag, and keep it in the freezer for up to 3 months. Use it a slice at a time for sandwiches or toast, or simply enjoy some with salad or soup. This bread also makes great croutons.

For instructions for making croutons, see page 195.

Nutrition Per Serving:
286 calories, 16g fat, 6g saturated fat, 50mg cholesterol, 454 mg sodium, 32g carbohydrate, 2g fiber, 5g protein

Recipe courtesy of Domata Living™

Feta-Basil Bread Ⓥ

Ingredients

¼ cup fresh basil leaves

¼ cup sun-dried tomatoes

2 cups Domata Living™ gluten-free all-purpose flour

3 tablespoons sugar

2½ teaspoons baking powder

½ teaspoon salt

1 cup feta cheese, crumbled

¾ cup whipping cream or heavy cream

⅓ cup half-and-half or light cream

⅓ cup canola oil

1 egg, beaten

Directions

1 Preheat oven to 400°F. Lightly grease a 9x5-inch loaf pan. Set aside.

2 To prepare fresh basil, wash basil leaves and pat dry. Remove stems. Fold leaves and chop into small pieces. See Photo A. To prepare dried tomatoes chop tomatoes into small pieces.

3 In a large bowl combine flour, sugar, baking powder, and salt. Add feta cheese, basil, and dried tomatoes. In a medium bowl beat together whipping cream, half-and-half, oil, and egg. Pour egg mixture into flour mixture, stirring until just moistened. See Photo B.

4 Transfer batter to prepared pan. See Photo C. Bake about 35 minutes or until a wooden toothpick when inserted in the center comes out clean. Cool in pan for 5 minutes. Remove from pan and cool on a wire rack. *Serves 10.*

> **Elizabeth says:**
> Unlike many gluten-free breads, this bread is moist and chewy because of the feta cheese and dried tomatoes. It's one of my favorites!

This versatile bread tastes great made into almost any kind of sandwich. Try it with thinly sliced roast beef, chipolte chile- or herb-seasoned mayonnaise, sliced tomatoes, and gluten-free olives.

Millet Flatbread **V** **LF** **WG**

Special Health Benefits

Nutritionally speaking, millet is similar to wheat. One-third cup of millet flour (35 grams) contains about 4 grams of protein, which is very close to wheat. A single serving has 15% of the US Recommended Daily Allowance (RDA) of iron, and is high in B vitamins, magnesium, and potassium.

Ingredients

- 2 teaspoons active dry yeast
- 1 teaspoon sugar
- ¼ cup lukewarm water (about 110°F)
- 1¼ cups millet flour
- ¾ cup tapioca flour
- 2 tablespoons sugar
- ½ teaspoon salt
- 2 eggs, beaten
- ½ cup milk
- 2 tablespoons olive oil
- 1 teaspoon gluten-free vinegar

Directions

1 Preheat oven to 200°F, then shut off oven immediately. Line a 15x10-inch jelly-roll pan with parchment paper. Set aside.

2 In a small bowl mix yeast and 1 teaspoon sugar; stir in lukewarm water. Let stand about 5 minutes or until bubbly and frothy. See Photo A.

3 In a large mixing bowl stir together millet flour, tapioca flour, 2 tablespoons sugar, and salt. In a medium bowl combine eggs, milk, oil, and vinegar. Stir yeast mixture into egg mixture.

4 Slowly pour egg mixture into dry ingredients. See Photo B. Using a mixer, beat for 3 to 5 minutes or until thoroughly combined. Batter will be thin and pourable. Pour batter onto parchment paper in jelly-roll pan and evenly spread over entire surface. See Photos C and D.

5 Cover and let rise in the warm oven for 40 to 50 minutes or until doubled. Remove from oven. Preheat oven to 425°F. Bake for 11 to 15 minutes or until bread is lightly browned on top. *Serves 15.*

Nutrition Per Serving:
77 calories, 3g fat, 0g saturated fat, 28mg cholesterol, 168mg sodium, 12g carbohydrate, 0g fiber, 2g protein

A

B

C

D

Although Millet Flatbread looks like other flatbreads, it's actually softer in texture. Serve it as a side with soups and stews, or top it with fresh mozzarella cheese and fresh basil for a quick snack.

Banana Bread

Special Health Benefits
Bananas are a nutrition bargain. With only 90 calories each, they are a great source of nutrients such as the B-complex vitamins, vitamin C, potassium, manganese, and magnesium. One banana also provides 11 percent of the daily recommended requirement of fiber.

Ingredients

3 ripe bananas
1 cup sugar
½ cup butter, softened
2 eggs
3 tablespoons buttermilk
1 teaspoon baking powder
1 teaspoon baking soda
½ teaspoon salt
2 cups gluten-free all-purpose flour such as Domata Living™ Flour

Directions

1 Preheat oven to 350°F. Grease a 9x5-inch loaf pan. Set aside. Peel and lay bananas in a shallow dish or plate. Using a fork, mash the bananas until all small pieces are softened. See Photo A.

2 In a large mixing bowl combine sugar and butter. Using a mixer, beat until creamy. See Photo B. Add eggs and mashed bananas. In a small bowl mix buttermilk, baking powder, baking soda, and salt. See Photo C. Add to butter mixture and mix well.

3 Add flour mixture to butter mixture and mix well. See Photo D. Pour into prepared loaf pan. Bake about 25 minutes or until a wooden toothpick comes out clean when inserted in the center. *Serves 10.*

Marcia says:

I make this bread to take to potlucks, family reunions, or other gatherings. Everyone loves it and few realize it's gluten-free.

Nutrition Per Serving:
327 calories, 11g fat, 6g saturated fat, 67 mg cholesterol, 317 mg sodium, 56g carbohydrate, 2g fiber, 4g protein

The bananas in this easy quick bread help keep it moist. For a ready-any-time snack, seal individual slices of the bread in small freezer bags and stash them in the freezer.

Cracked Rice Bread Ⓥ ⓁⒻ Ⓦⓖ

**Plan Ahead
and Save Time**

*If you have a few
extra minutes, crack
the rice for this
bread recipe ahead
of time. Keep it in a
tightly covered jar in
the refrigerator until
you're ready to use
it. The cracked rice
will last for about
two weeks.*

Freeze for Later

*This bread freezes
well sliced or whole.
It will keep for up
to 2 months in your
freezer.*

Ingredients

4½ teaspoons rapid rise
active dry yeast

2 teaspoons sugar

1 cup warm milk

⅓ cup brown rice

1 cups sweet white
sorghum flour

1 cup all-purpose flour
such as Namaste®
Perfect Flour Blend

1 tablespoon packed
brown sugar

1 teaspoon salt

½ cup soft silken tofu

1 egg

3 tablespoons
vegetable oil

Directions

1 Grease a 9x5-inch loaf pan. Set aside. In a small
bowl mix yeast and 2 teaspoons sugar; stir in
warm milk. Let stand about 5 minutes or until
bubbly and frothy. See Photo A.

2 In a food processor or coffee grinder crack brown
rice into small pieces. See Photo B. Set aside. In
a large mixing bowl stir together the processed
brown rice, sorghum flour, all-purpose flour, brown
sugar, and salt.

3 Transfer tofu to a small bowl; measure tofu. See
Photo C. Place tofu in a medium bowl. Add egg
and oil and beat until smooth.

4 Pour tofu mixture into dry ingredients. See
Photo D. Using a mixer on low speed, beat until
combined. Add yeast mixture and beat on high
speed for 2 minutes. See Photo E. Pour batter into
prepared pan.

5 Cover and let rise in a warm place for 45 to
60 minutes or until doubled. Batter will look very
light. See Photo F. Preheat oven to 350°F. Bake for
40 to 50 minutes or until top is golden brown. Cool
in pan for 5 minutes. Remove from pan and cool
on a wire rack. *Serves 10.*

**Nutrition
Per Serving:**
252 calories, 6g fat,
1g saturated fat,
22mg cholesterol,
258mg sodium,
45g carbohydrate,
3g fiber, 7g protein

Carol says:
We wanted to create
a loaf that was
similar to a whole
wheat bread, making
delightfully crunchy
toast. This cracked
rice bread is it!

A   B   C

Serve as bread or toast with soup or salad and enjoy the crunchiness that it lends to the meal.

D   E   F

Cranberry-Applesauce Muffins Ⓥ ⑤ ⑥

**Special
Health Benefits**

*Little but luscious,
cranberries are
packed with good
nutrition. They are
high in vitamin C
and fiber. Like their
relative the blueberry,
cranberries also
contain antioxidants in
abundance which help
the body fight disease.*

Ingredients

1 cup fresh or frozen cranberries

1¼ cups unsweetened applesauce

⅓ cup canola oil

1 egg, beaten

2 cups gluten-free all-purpose flour such as Domata Living™ Flour

½ cup sugar

1 teaspoon baking soda

1 teaspoon ground cinnamon

½ teaspoon salt

Directions

1 Preheat oven to 350°F. Grease 24 muffin cups. Set aside. Using a food processor, process cranberries until chopped. Set aside.

2 In a small bowl mix applesauce, oil, and egg. In a large bowl combine flour, sugar, baking soda, cinnamon, and salt. Make a well in the dry ingredients. Slowly pour in egg mixture, stirring until just moistened. Fold in cranberries.

3 Fill prepared muffins cups two-thirds full. Bake for 25 to 30 minutes or until a wooden toothpick comes out clean inserted in the center. Cool for 2 minutes before removing from cups.
Serves 24.

Some gluten-free muffins are dry and crumbly—but not these colorful cranberry beauties. The applesauce keeps them deliciously moist.

**Nutrition
Per Serving:**
101 calories, 3g fat,
0g saturated fat,
9mg cholesterol,
107mg sodium,
17g carbohydrate,
1g fiber, 1g protein

Jalapeño Corn Muffins **V** **WG**

Ingredients

2¾ cups gluten-free all-purpose flour such as Domata Living™ Flour

¾ cup sugar

⅔ cup yellow cornmeal

2 teaspoons salt

1 teaspoon baking powder

1½ cups buttermilk

4 eggs, beaten

¾ cup vegetable oil

⅔ cup shredded cheddar cheese

4 jalapeño peppers, seeded and chopped

Directions

1 Preheat oven to 375°F. Grease 24 muffin cups. Set aside. In a large bowl combine flour, sugar, cornmeal, salt, and baking powder. Make a well in the dry ingredients. Set aside.

2 In a small bowl mix buttermilk, eggs, and oil. Slowly pour egg mixture into dry ingredients, stirring until just moistened. Fold in cheese and jalapeño peppers.

3 Fill prepared muffin cups three-fourths full. Bake for 20 to 25 minutes or until golden brown and firm in the center. *Serves 24.*

Freeze for Later
Delicious with chili and other full-flavored main dishes, these muffins freeze very well. Cool the baked muffins completely and place them in a freezer container deep enough so the muffins can stand upright and maintain their shape. Store in the freezer for up to 3 months.

Little bits of jalapeño pepper add just the right amount of zip and color to these delicate corn muffins.

Nutrition Per Serving:
193 calories, 9g fat, 2g saturated fat, 24mg cholesterol, 268mg sodium, 24g carbohydrate, 1g fiber, 4g protein

Maple-Walnut Bran Muffins V LF WG

**Special
Health Benefits**

*Even though the
name may imply it,
buckwheat is not
related to wheat.
Buckwheat is actually
a fruit seed that is
related to rhubarb and
sorrel. The protein in
buckwheat contains
eight essential amino
acids and is high in
lysine. Buckwheat
is also rich in many
B vitamins as well
as phosphorus,
magnesium, iron,
zinc, copper, and
manganese.*

Ingredients

1   cup buckwheat flour
1   cup tapioca flour
1   teaspoon baking soda
¼   teaspoon salt
½   cup rice bran
2   bananas, mashed
⅔   cup buttermilk
½   cup gluten-free
     maple syrup
¼   cup oil
1   egg, beaten
⅔   cup walnuts

Directions

1 Preheat oven to 350°F. Grease 18 muffin cups. Set aside. In a large mixing bowl mix buckwheat flour, tapioca flour, baking soda, and salt. Add rice bran and mix well. See Photo A. Make a well in the dry ingredients. Set aside.

2 In a medium bowl mix bananas, buttermilk, maple syrup, oil, and egg. Slowly pour egg mixture into dry ingredients. See Photo B. Stir until just moistened. Fold in walnuts. See Photo C.

3 Fill prepared muffin cups two-thirds full. Bake about 20 minutes or until a wooden toothpick comes out clean inserted in the center. *Serves 18.*

> **Elizabeth says:**
> Using rice bran instead of wheat bran gives these gluten-free muffins the same texture as a wheat bran muffin.

**Nutrition
Per Serving:**
164 calories, 7g fat,
1g saturated fat,
24mg cholesterol,
121mg sodium,
24g carbohydrate,
3g fiber, 3g protein

A   B   C

Enjoying bran muffins doesn't have to be a thing of the past just because you're eating gluten-free. Give these rice bran muffins a try. Maple syrup, bananas, and walnuts make them a cut above the rest.

Homestyle Waffles **V** **LF**

Add a Flavor Variation

If you like fruity waffles, add a mix of finely chopped apples and walnuts to the dry ingredients before mixing. Or add fresh or dried blueberries or dried currants to the batter before cooking.

Ingredients

1½ cups gluten-free all-purpose flour such as Namaste® Perfect Flour Blend

2 tablespoons sugar

1 tablespoon baking powder

½ teaspoon salt

2 cups milk

1 egg

3 tablespoons butter, melted

Other suggested toppings:

Whipped cream

Fresh fruit

Crumbled cooked bacon

Marmalade or preserves

Powdered sugar

Directions

1 In a large bowl mix the flour, sugar, baking powder, and salt. Make a well in the dry ingredients. Set aside.

2 In a large, glass measuring cup mix the milk, egg, and melted butter. Pour egg mixture into dry ingredients. See Photo A.

3 Beat batter with a whisk until just combined. Batter will be lumpy and thick. See Photo B.

4 Preheat a greased waffle iron. Pour or scoop batter onto the iron in a circle, using about ¾ cup batter for each waffle. See Photo C. Cook waffle until brown or as indicated by light on the waffle iron. Remove waffle from iron. *Serves 6.*

Marcia says:

I make these waffles all the time! We enjoy them for breakfast, lunch, or dinner, even reheating the leftovers.

Nutrition Per Serving:

346 calories, 7g fat, 4g saturated fat, 52mg cholesterol, 497mg sodium, 63g carbohydrate, 3g fiber, 8g protein

A

B

C

Take your pick. Serve these waffles plain with butter and a drizzle of gluten-free maple syrup, or dress them up with whipped cream, fresh fruit, and a dusting of powdered sugar.

Tuscan Flatbread Ⓥ ㉫ ㊎

Add a Flavor Variation

Choose your favorite spice or herb to add to this flatbread. Substitute oregano or parsley for the basil. Or create a seasoning such as thyme, basil, and oregano mixed with a dash of cayenne pepper or cumin.

Ingredients

1 cup lukewarm water (about 110°F)

2 packages quick-rise active dry yeast

1 tablespoon butter, melted

1½ cups gluten-free all-purpose flour such as Namaste® Perfect Flour Blend

½ cup corn flour or Masa Harina flour

2 tablespoons millet flour

1 tablespoon sugar

1 tablespoon chopped fresh basil

1 teaspoon salt

¼ cup olive oil

2 teaspoons coarse sea salt

Directions

1 In a large mixing bowl stir lukewarm water into yeast until dissolved. Let stand for 5 minutes. Stir in melted butter.

2 In a small mixing bowl stir together all-purpose flour, corn flour, millet flour, sugar, basil, and 1 teaspoon salt. Add the yeast mixture to dry ingredients and mix well. See Photo A.

3 Cover and let rise in a warm place about 30 minutes or until doubled. Divide into thirds. Pat out each portion on a large cookie sheet. Make indentations with thumb. See Photo B.

4 Preheat oven to 400°F. Use a pastry brush to brush dough with oil. See Photo C. Sprinkle with coarse salt. See Photo D. Bake about 25 minutes or until golden brown. Remove bread from pan and cool on wire racks. Break into pieces. *Serves 12.*

Nutrition Per Serving:

256 calories, 9g fat, 2g saturated fat, 4mg cholesterol, 449mg sodium, 41g carbohydrate, 3g fiber, 4g protein

Round out your next Italian meal with this delectable flatbread. Don't forget to set out some olive oil sprinkled with grated Parmesan cheese and cracked black pepper for dipping.

Cinnamon Rolls **V EF**

Plan Ahead and Save Time

You can enjoy these yummy yeast rolls in the morning fresh out of the oven if you do a little prep work the night before. In a glass measuring cup combine the milk, the 3 tablespoons sugar, oil, and honey. Cover and store in the refrigerator. In a small mixing bowl combine the flour, salt, and baking powder. Cover; set aside. Finally, assemble the ¾ cup sugar and cinnamon. Cover; set aside. Come morning, much of the work will be done.

Ingredients

¾ cup lukewarm water (about 110°F)

2 packages active dry yeast

¾ cup milk

3 tablespoons sugar

2 tablespoons canola oil

1 tablespoon honey

3½ cups gluten-free all-purpose flour such as Domata Living™ Flour

2 teaspoons salt

1 teaspoon baking powder

¼ cup carbonated water

¾ cup sugar

3 tablespoons ground cinnamon

½ cup butter, cut into 12 squares

Pecan halves (optional)

Directions

1 Preheat oven to 375°F. Grease 6 large muffin cups or 12 regular-sized muffin cups. Set aside. In a large mixing bowl stir lukewarm water into yeast until dissolved. Add milk, 3 tablespoons sugar, oil, and honey and mix well. See Photo A. Let stand for 5 minutes.

2 In a small mixing bowl combine flour, salt, and baking powder. Add flour mixture to milk mixture and beat until combined. See Photo B. Stir in carbonated water. Fill muffin cups about half full.

3 In a small bowl mix ¾ cup sugar and cinnamon. Sprinkle batter in each cup with about 1 tablespoon sugar mixture; top with a square of butter. See Photo C. Fill with remaining batter. See Photo D.

4 Use a large skewer to make a swirl in the top of batter in each cup. See Photo E. Top with remaining sugar mixture and remaining butter. Bake about 20 minutes or until golden brown. Top with pecan halves if desired. *Serves 12.*

Nutrition Per Serving:

315 calories, 10g fat, 5g saturated fat, 20 mg cholesterol, 446 mg sodium, 53g carbohydrate, 2g fiber, 4g protein

You'll be amazed that rolls that are so soft and sweet can be a part of a gluten-free diet. Pop a batch in the oven and the wonderful aroma will bring everyone running to the kitchen to see what's baking.

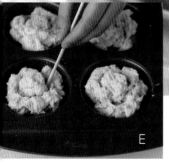

E

Breads are one of the most desired

products for individuals on a gluten-free diet, but unfortunately they are also one of the most challenging gluten-free products to make. Yeast bread is especially challenging to make without gluten. That is because gluten has very specific functions in yeast bread; it is required for the elasticity and stretchiness of the dough, and it traps gases in the bread for lightness. When making yeast bread, remember that you must have four essential ingredients: yeast, flour, liquid, and salt. Yeast produces carbon dioxide to leaven the bread, but salt prevents the yeast from producing carbon dioxide too rapidly. Without gluten, it is much more difficult to trap the carbon dioxide in the bread, so gluten-free yeast bread often collapses or does not rise. If you are trying to make a yeast bread into a gluten-free recipe, try these tips:

- Replace water with carbonated water to add bubbles of carbon dioxide in the bread. Always use a fresh bottle of carbonated water to get maximum effect.

- Use a low mixing speed when stirring the bread.

- Increase the amount of yeast to create more carbon dioxide. Don't increase the amount of yeast by more than 25%, or the bread may have a yeasty flavor.

- Let the bread rise in a warm, humid environment. Try putting the bread in a slightly warm oven with a tray of water in the bottom of the oven.

Carol says:

In developing recipes with gluten-free all-purpose flour as a main ingredient, it was amazing how each mix had their own characteristics and how the final result varied greatly depending on which flour combination we used.

5 Hearty Soups

Butternut Squash Soup V LF EF

Special Health Benefits

Winter squash, such as butternut or acorn squash, is full of valuable nutrition. It is high in vitamins A and C as well as in potassium. This inexpensive vegetable is available nearly all year long.

So beautiful to look at and elegant to serve, this soup is a delicious way to start a meal. Vary the flavor by sprinkling it with nutmeg, cinnamon, or curry powder.

Ingredients

1 cup water

1 2- to 3-pound butternut squash

3 tablespoons butter

¼ cup thinly sliced shallots or green onions

5 to 6 cups gluten-free chicken broth such as Better Than Bouillon®

Salt and pepper

Ground nutmeg, ground cinnamon, or curry powder (optional)

Directions

1 Preheat oven to 375°F. Grease a 13x9-inch baking pan; add water. Cut squash in half lengthwise. Using a large spoon, remove seeds. Place squash halves, cut sides down, in pan. Bake, covered, about 45 minutes or until a fork inserted in thickest part of squash enters easily. Cool in pan about 20 minutes or until cool to the touch. Remove peel from squash and place flesh in a large bowl.

2 In a large saucepan melt butter. Add shallots and cook about 5 minutes or until tender. Add chicken broth. Bring to boiling; reduce heat to medium. Stir in squash.

3 Transfer about half of the mixture to a blender and puree until smooth. Pour into a large bowl. Repeat with remaining mixture. Add salt and pepper to taste. Ladle into bowls. If desired, top with nutmeg, cinnamon, or curry powder. *Serves 8.*

Nutrition Per Serving:
103 calories, 4g fat, 3g saturated fat, 11mg cholesterol, 353mg sodium, 15g carbohydrate, 0g fiber, 3g protein

Chicken Noodle Soup LF HP

Ingredients

2 tablespoons butter

¼ cup chopped celery

1 tablespoon sliced green onion

4 cups gluten-free chicken broth such as Better Than Bouillon®

1 cup sliced carrots

½ recipe Gluten-Free Noodles (see page 16)

2 cups chopped cooked chicken

1 tablespoon chopped fresh parsley

Directions

1 In a large saucepan melt butter. Add celery and onion. Cook, covered, on medium-low heat about 5 minutes or until tender.

2 Add chicken broth and bring to boiling. Add carrots and reduce heat. Simmer for 5 minutes.

3 Return broth mixture to boiling and add Gluten-Free Noodles. Cook about 5 minutes or until noodles are tender. Stir in chicken and parsley. Cook for 1 minute more. *Serves 6.*

Special Health Benefits

Cooking raw vegetables directly in the broth, as in this chicken soup, captures more of the vitamins than cooking the vegetables separately. Many vitamins leach out into the cooking water, so by using only one pan you are guaranteed to keep more vitamins in the soup.

When the cold winds blow or you're simply feeling under the weather, nothing comforts more than a steaming bowl of this chunky soup.

Nutrition Per Serving:
155 calories, 3g fat, 1g saturated fat, 89mg cholesterol, 625mg sodium, 14g carbohydrate, 1g fiber, 18g protein

Easy Chili (LF) (HP) (CF) (EF)

Read the Label

When you're choosing salsa, picante sauce, or a similar product, make sure you read the label carefully. Look for words such as "food starch", or "emulsifiers." These general terms may mean that there is gluten in the product. See page 188 for more help with reading labels. If you're still unsure, call the company or check its web site.

Diced tomatoes and gluten-free salsa help you put together this zesty chili in minutes.

Ingredients

1 pound lean ground beef

Salt and pepper

1 28-ounce can diced tomatoes, undrained

1 24-ounce jar gluten-free salsa such as Pace® Picante Salsa

1 15-ounce can gluten-free chili beans, black beans, or kidney beans, undrained

Shredded cheese (optional)

Directions

1 In a medium skillet brown ground beef on medium-high heat. Drain beef. Set aside.

2 In a large saucepan combine tomatoes with juice, salsa, and beans with liquid. Bring to boiling; reduce heat. Simmer for 5 minutes. Stir in ground beef. Return to boiling; reduce heat. Simmer for 20 minutes, stirring occasionally. Add salt and pepper to taste.

3 Ladle chili into bowls. If desired, top with cheese. *Serves 5.*

Marcia says:
This is my go-to supper. I always keep the ingredients on hand so I can make it at the last minute. It's a favorite for the whole family!

Nutrition Per Serving:
224 calories, 4g fat, 2g saturated fat, 46mg cholesterol, 898mg sodium, 25g carbohydrate, 7g fiber, 22g protein

French Onion Soup HP EF

Ingredients

2 tablespoons butter

2 cups thinly sliced yellow onions (2 large)

4 cups gluten-free beef broth such as Better Than Bouillon®

¼ teaspoon pepper

2 cups mashed potatoes

1 tablespoon cornstarch

2 tablespoons butter

1 cup shredded Swiss, Gruyère, or Jarlsberg cheese (4 ounces)

Directions

1 In a large saucepan melt 2 tablespoons butter; add onions. Cook, covered, on medium-low heat for 8 to 10 minutes or until onions are tender and golden, stirring occasionally. Add beef broth and pepper. Bring to boiling; reduce heat. Simmer, covered, for 10 minutes.

2 Meanwhile, preheat broiler. In a medium bowl combine mashed potatoes and cornstarch. Form potato mixture into four patties. In a large skillet melt 2 tablespoons butter on medium-high heat. Add patties and cook until heated through and brown on both sides.

3 To serve, ladle soup into oven-safe ramekins and place in a shallow baking pan. Top with cheese. Broil just until cheese is melted. Top with hot potato patties. Serve immediately. *Serves 4.*

Read the Label

When shopping for beef and chicken broth, don't let the variety of products confuse you. Available in boxes, jars, and cans as well as in bouillon cubes or granules, many beef and chicken broth products contain gluten. Always read the label looking for words such as "caramelized color" or "modified food starch."

Left-over mashed potatoes fried in butter are a tasty gluten-free substitute for croutons in this tempting version of the classic soup.

Nutrition Per Serving:
345 calories, 20g fat, 13g saturated fat, 57mg cholesterol, 1155mg sodium, 29g carbohydrate, 3g fiber, 13g protein

Read the Label

When it comes to gluten-free pastas, you'll find they are made from several different grains.

The most common gluten-free pastas use brown rice, corn, and/ or quinoa flours. All have slightly different textures, flavors, and cooking instructions. Be sure to follow the directions carefully for each type.

Garbanzo Bean Soup   Ⓥ ⓁⒻ ⒽⓅ ⒸⒻ

Ingredients

2   tablespoons olive oil

1   small onion, chopped

1   14.5-ounce can petite diced tomatoes, undrained, or 1½ cups peeled and diced fresh tomatoes

2   cups gluten-free chicken broth such as Better Than Bouillon®

1   15.8-ounce can garbanzo beans, rinsed and drained

2   tablespoons chopped fresh basil

1   8-ounce package gluten-free elbow-style corn pasta

Shredded Parmesan cheese (optional)

Directions

1 In a large saucepan heat olive oil on medium heat. Add onion and cook until tender. See Photo A.

2 Add tomatoes with juice and cook for 5 minutes, stirring occasionally. See Photo B.

3 Add chicken broth, garbanzo beans, and basil. Bring to boiling; reduce heat. Simmer, covered, for 5 minutes. See Photo C.

4 Meanwhile, cook pasta as directed on package. Drain well. Add to tomato mixture and stir to combine. See Photo D.

5 Ladle soup into bowls. Top with Parmesan cheese. *Serves 8.*

Elizabeth says:

The combination of flavors and textures in this soup will please even the most finicky eater. It is one of my favorite soups!

Nutrition Per Serving:
229 calories, 6g fat, 1g saturated fat, 3mg cholesterol, 373mg sodium, 39g carbohydrate, 6g fiber, 8g protein

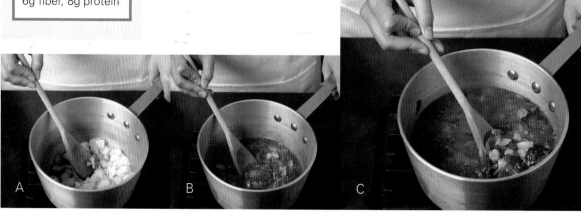

A   B   C

Serve this awesome bean-and-pasta soup with fried corn sticks. To make the corn sticks, cut Buttery Corn Bread (see page 81) into narrow rectangles and fry the pieces in a little butter.

Beef-Vegetable Soup **LF** **HP** **CF** **EF**

Freeze for Later

Making your own beef or chicken stock assures you that it's gluten-free. Make the stock ahead of time so it's ready and waiting in the freezer. Freeze recipe-size portions of stock in freezer containers and keep them in the freezer for up to 6 months. To use the stock, thaw it overnight in the refrigerator or in the microwave oven.

This stick-to-the-ribs soup owes its appealing mix of colors and flavors to carrots, sweet potato, corn, peas, green beans, and red cabbage.

Nutrition Per Serving:
124 calories, 5g fat, 2g saturated fat, 24mg cholesterol, 331mg sodium, 10g carbohydrate, 2g fiber, 10g protein

Ingredients

3   pounds beef shanks or 1 large soup bone
6   cups water
1   medium onion, chopped
1   stalk celery, chopped
1   teaspoon salt
1   teaspoon pepper
1   cup sliced carrots
1   cup chopped peeled sweet potato
½ cup *each* frozen corn, peas, and cut green beans
¼ cup chopped red cabbage

Directions

1 To make beef stock, place beef shanks or soup bone in a stockpot and add water, onion, celery, salt, and pepper. Bring to boiling; reduce heat. Simmer, covered, about 1 hour or until meat is falling off the bones. Remove meat from broth and set aside in a bowl. Remove meat from bones; discard bones. Cover and refrigerate meat until ready to use. Strain cooking liquid into a bowl and cool in refrigerator. Skim off fat.

2 Transfer stock to a large saucepan. Add carrots and sweet potato. Bring to boiling; reduce heat. Simmer, covered, about 15 minutes or until tender.

3 Stir in meat, frozen vegetables, cabbage, and, if desired, salt and pepper to taste. Return to boiling; reduce heat. Simmer about 5 minutes more or until vegetables are tender. *Serves 8.*

Tomato-Basil Soup ⓋⓈⓅ

Ingredients

3 tablespoons butter

¼ cup chopped green onions

¼ cup chopped celery

1 cup gluten-free chicken broth such as Better Than Bouillon®

¼ cup cold water

1 tablespoon cornstarch

2 14.5-ounce cans diced tomatoes, undrained

1 tablespoon chopped fresh basil or 1 teaspoon dried basil

1 recipe Gluten--Free Croutons (see page 195) (optional)

Shredded Pepper Jack cheese

Directions

1 In a large saucepan melt butter. Add green onions and celery and cook until tender.

2 Add chicken broth to saucepan. Bring to boiling and boil for 1 minute. In a small bowl mix water and cornstarch; stir into broth mixture. Boil for 1 minute more.

3 Stir in tomatoes with juice and basil. Return to boiling; reduce heat. Simmer for 5 minutes.

4 Ladle soup into cups or bowls. Top with Gluten--Free Croutons (if desired) and cheese. *Serves 6.*

The Cost

Canned tomatoes are inexpensive and versatile to use in so many recipes. They help keep the cost of this entire recipe down to about $4.00—less than $1.00 per serving.

For a fantastic yet simple supper, team this satisfying soup with your favorite gluten-free sandwich or omelet.

Nutrition Per Serving:
105 calories, 7g fat, 5g saturated fat, 19mg cholesterol, 138mg sodium, 8g carbohydrate, 2g fiber, 3g protein

New England Clam Chowder HP EF

Where to Find It

You'll find shucked fresh clams at a local seafood shop or in the fish department of large supermarkets. When shopping for clams, look for plump pieces in a clear liquid. The clams should have a fresh scent (not sour or fishy). When you get the clams home, refrigerate them in their liquor for up to 2 days or freeze them for 3 months.

Ingredients

1 pint shucked clams or two 6.5-ounce cans minced clams, undrained

1 tablespoon lemon juice

½ cup chopped onion

2 slices bacon, chopped

3 cups chopped peeled potatoes (about 3 large)

1 tablespoon concentrated gluten-free chicken bouillon such as Better Than Bouillon®

¼ teaspoon dried thyme

¼ teaspoon pepper

2½ cups whole milk

½ cup half-and-half or light cream

2 tablespoons cornstarch

Directions

1 Chop fresh clams, reserving juice; set clams aside. Strain clam juice to remove bits of shell; measure 1 cup juice. Or drain canned clams, reserving 1 cup juice. Add lemon juice to clam juice. Set aside.

2 In a large saucepan cook onion and bacon on medium heat until bacon is crisp. See Photo A. Stir in potatoes.

3 In a glass measuring cup mix the reserved clam juice, bouillon, thyme, and pepper. Pour into bacon mixture. See Photo B. Bring to boiling; reduce heat. Simmer, covered, about 10 minutes or until potatoes are tender. Using a fork, mash potatoes slightly against side of pan. See Photo C.

4 In a glass measuring cup mix milk, half-and-half, and cornstarch. Pour into potato mixture. See Photo D. Cook and stir until thickened and bubbly. Stir in clams. See Photo E. Cook for 1 to 2 minutes more or until heated through. *Serves 8.*

Nutrition Per Serving:
270 calories, 9g fat, 3g saturated fat, 77mg cholesterol, 329mg sodium, 22g carbohydrate, 1g fiber, 29g protein

A

B

C

D

Made with both milk and half-and-half, this thick, rich soup is a true New England chowder. For a satisfying meal, serve it with slabs of Tuscan Flatbread (see page 96).

Split Pea Soup (LF) (HP) (EF)

**Special
Health Benefits**

*Split peas are in
the legume family,
the same family as
beans and lentils.
They are a good
source of protein
with 16 grams in
1 cup. This provides
roughly 33 percent of
the daily requirement
for protein for only
231 calories. They're
also a great source
of potassium and
dietary fiber.*

Ingredients

2 tablespoons butter

1¼ cups sliced carrots

1 cup chopped onion

1 cup chopped celery

4 cups gluten-free
chicken broth such as
Better Than Bouillon®

2 cups water

1 cup dried green split
peas, rinsed and
drained

2 cups diced gluten-free
ham

2 cups frozen peas

1 tablespoon butter

Salt and pepper

Gluten-free dairy sour
cream (optional)

Directions

1 In a large saucepan melt 2 tablespoons butter.
Add carrots, onion, and celery. Cook, covered,
on medium-high heat for 3 to 4 minutes or until
vegetables are soft. See Photo A.

2 Add broth, water, and split peas. See Photo B.

3 Bring to boiling; reduce heat. Simmer, partially
covered, for 50 to 60 minutes or until split peas are
tender. See Photo C. Stir in ham, frozen peas, and
1 tablespoon butter. Add salt and pepper to taste.

4 Ladle soup into bowls. If desired, serve with sour
cream. *Serves 6.*

Carol says:
The combination of dried split
peas and frozen green peas
gives this soup fabulous texture
and color. The ham adds a
captivating hint of smokiness.

**Nutrition
Per Serving:**
262 calories, 7g fat,
4g saturated fat,
25mg cholesterol,
588mg sodium, 33g
carbohydrate, 12g
fiber, 17g protein

A

B

C

Blustery days are just meant for soup. So when the weather puts you in the mood for a full-flavored bowl of something good, dish up this rich, veggie-filled soup. Add a crisp lettuce salad and the meal is complete.

For individuals on a gluten-free diet,

it can be very difficult to get a mix of essential nutrients from one meal. Soups, however, offer a great way to consume protein, carbohydrates, fatty acids, vitamins, and minerals. Because soup combines so many different ingredients, it is a great all-in-one nutritious meal. In addition, homemade soups are very inexpensive, easy-to-make, and many can be made in under 30 minutes. Soups are also a great way to use leftovers. By simply chopping up a cooked beef roast, cubing cooked chicken, or slicing vegetables, you already have some of the ingredients you need—and you have saved money. Try these tips to increase the variety of nutrients you eat in one soup:

> **Marcia says:**
> I often make my own broth and keep it in the freezer to have on hand to make soups and casseroles. I freeze it in small containers and mark the date it was made. Look at the directions for the Vegetable Beef Soup on page 108 for tips on making your own homemade beef broth.

- By making your own broth for soup, you can drastically decrease the amount of sodium in the soup, increase the amount of nutrients, and guarantee it is gluten-free. Homemade broth is also cheaper than purchased broth and very easy to make.

- Add a variety of colors of vegetables to increase the amount of nutrients. In general, orange vegetables such as carrots and sweet potatoes will add vitamin A, green vegetables such as broccoli will add vitamin K and calcium, and red vegetables such as tomatoes will add vitamin C.

- For a soup lower in fat, choose a broth-based soup instead of a cream-based soup. Also, when possible, substitute nonfat milk for whole milk in cream soups.

6 Cookies, Cakes, and Candies

Coconut Cake Ⓥ Ⓦⓖ

Where to Find It

Don't confuse coconut milk with coconut cream. Coconut milk is made from a mixture of water and coconut pulp. Coconut cream is sweet and very thick and is used primarily for desserts and beverages. Look for coconut milk in the Asian food section of the supermarket or at Asian food markets.

6

Nutrition Per Serving:
555 calories, 20g fat, 9g saturated fat, 54mg cholesterol, 173mg sodium, 94g carbohydrate, 1g fiber, 5g protein

Ingredients
- 2 eggs
- 1 cup sugar
- ½ cup milk
- ½ cup coconut milk
- 6 tablespoons shredded coconut
- ¼ cup canola oil
- 3 tablespoons grated Parmesan cheese
- 1 cup corn flour
- 1½ teaspoons baking powder
- 1 cup shredded coconut
- 1 recipe Coconut Frosting

Directions
1 Preheat oven to 325°F. Grease an 8x8-inch baking pan and dust with corn flour. Set aside. In a large mixing bowl beat eggs with an electric mixer until they begin to foam. See Photo A.

2 Add sugar and beat well. Add milk, coconut milk, 6 tablespoons coconut, oil, and cheese. See Photo B. Beat until combined.

3 Mix corn flour and baking powder and add to egg mixture. Mix well. See Photo C. Pour into prepared pan. Bake about 45 minutes or until top is golden and a wooden toothpick comes out clean when inserted in the center. Cool on a wire rack.

4 Meanwhile, to toast the 1 cup coconut, preheat broiler. Evenly spread coconut onto a baking sheet. Broil about 1 minute or until coconut is just beginning to brown on the top. Coconut will burn easily, so watch carefully. Cool.

5 Frost cake with Coconut Frosting. *Serves 9.*

Coconut Frosting
1 In a medium bowl beat together ¼ cup softened butter and ¼ cup milk. Gradually add 4 cups powdered sugar, beating until creamy. Sprinkle with toasted coconut after frosting cake.

A

B   C

Believe it or not, Parmesan cheese is the secret to this rich, moist cake's extraordinary flavor. Serve it with tea or coffee for an afternoon treat or after-dinner dessert.

Chocolate Chip Cookies ⓥ

Freeze for Later

Keep a supply of these scrumptious cookies in the freezer for spur-of-the-moment snacks or desserts. Seal the cooled cookies in freezer bags and place them in the freezer. They'll last for up to 3 months, but chances are your family will enjoy them long before then.

6

Packed with chocolate chips and walnuts, these family-pleasing classics just have to be enjoyed with a glass of cold milk.

Ingredients

2¼ cups gluten-free all-purpose flour such as Domata Living™ Flour

1 teaspoon baking soda

1 teaspoon salt

1 cup butter, softened

¾ cup granulated sugar

¾ cup packed brown sugar

1 teaspoon vanilla

2 eggs

2 cups gluten-free semisweet chocolate chips

¼ cup chopped walnuts

Directions

1 Preheat oven to 375°F. In a small bowl combine flour, baking soda, and salt. Set aside.

2 In a large mixing bowl beat butter, granulated sugar, brown sugar, and vanilla with an electric mixer until creamy. Add eggs, one at a time, beating well after each addition. Gradually stir in flour mixture until blended. Stir in chocolate chips and walnuts.

3 Drop dough by rounded tablespoon onto a greased cookie sheet. Bake about 10 minutes or until golden brown. Cool on a wire rack or waxed paper. *Serves 24.*

Nutrition Per Serving:
270 calories, 12g fat, 5g saturated fat, 29mg cholesterol, 175mg sodium, 38g carbohydrate, 1g fiber, 2g protein

Fall Harvest Cake Ⓥ Ⓒ𝐅

Ingredients

1 ½ cups granulated sugar

½ cup packed brown sugar

2 teaspoons *each* baking soda and ground cinnamon

½ teaspoon salt

¼ teaspoon *each* ground nutmeg and ginger

1 15-ounce can pumpkin

4 eggs

1 cup canola oil

½ teaspoon vanilla

2 cups sifted Domata Living™ gluten-free all-purpose flour

1 large apple, peeled and chopped

½ cup chopped pecans

Directions

1 Preheat oven to 350°F. Grease and flour a 10-inch fluted tube pan; set aside. In a large bowl mix granulated sugar, brown sugar, baking soda, cinnamon, salt, nutmeg, and ginger. Stir in pumpkin, eggs, oil, and vanilla. Stir in flour, ½ cup at a time. Fold in apple and pecans. Pour into prepared pan.

2 Bake for 60 to 70 minutes or until a wooden toothpick comes out clean inserted near the center. Cool in pan for 10 minutes. Remove from pan and cool on a wire rack. *Serves 12.*

Marcia says:

When my family first tasted this spicy cake, we could hardly believe it could be so good yet still be gluten-free. Besides making it for dessert, I serve it for brunch without the whipped cream.

Special Health Benefits

The pumpkin in this tender cake brings you lots of terrific nutrition. Besides being low in fat and sodium, pumpkin is a good source of vitamins A and C, B vitamins, potassium, copper, and manganese.

Just like pumpkin pie, this rich cake gets its glorious flavor from an assortment of spices. Dress it up with whipped cream, apple slices, and a dusting of powdered sugar.

Nutrition Per Serving:

440 calories, 21g fat, 2g saturated fat, 70mg cholesterol, 425mg sodium, 61g carbohydrate, 3g fiber, 4g protein

Recipe courtesy of Domata Living™

Sugar Cookies 🅥 🅛🅕

Freeze for Later

No matter what the holiday—Halloween, Christmas, Valentine's Day, or Easter—these cookies are a great way to celebrate. Get a head start on the festivities by keeping an unfrosted batch or two in the freezer. (They will keep for up to 3 months.) When the holiday rolls around, thaw the cookies. Then frost and decorate them to suit the season.

Ingredients

5 tablespoons dairy sour cream

1 teaspoon baking soda

1 cup butter, softened

1 cup granulated sugar

1 egg

1 teaspoon vanilla

½ teaspoon salt

4½ cups gluten-free all-purpose flour such as Domata Living™ Flour

1 recipe Powdered Sugar Icing

Sanding sugar (optional)

Directions

1 Preheat oven to 350°F. Mix sour cream and baking soda. Set aside. In a large bowl beat butter and granulated sugar with electric mixer until creamy. Beat in egg, vanilla, salt, and sour cream mixture. Add flour, ½ cup at at time, beating until combined.

2 On a pastry cloth or board, roll out dough and cut into desired shapes. Place on an greased cookie sheet. Bake for 10 to 12 minutes or until lightly browned. Cool on a wire rack or waxed paper. Frost with Powdered Sugar Icing. If desired, sprinkle with sanding sugar. Makes 48 cookies. *Serves 24.*

Powdered Sugar Icing

1 In a medium bowl mix 4 cups powdered sugar, 2 tablespoons softened butter, and 1 teaspoon vanilla. Mix in enough milk (about 3 tablespoons) to make spreadable consistency.

Pretty to look at and yummy to eat, these cookies will disappear like magic once you put them in the cookie jar.

Nutrition Per Serving:

220 calories, 8g fat, 2g saturated fat, 18mg cholesterol, 164mg sodium, 32g carbohydrate, 2g fiber, 2g protein

Blonde Brownies

Ingredients

1 cup all-purpose gluten-free flour such as Bob's Red Mill®

2 teaspoons baking powder

½ teaspoon salt

½ cup butter

1 cup packed brown sugar

1 egg, beaten

1 teaspoon vanilla

Directions

1 Preheat oven to 350°F. Grease an 8x8-inch baking pan. Set aside.

2 In a small bowl stir together flour, baking powder, and salt. In a medium saucepan heat butter on low heat until melted. Remove from heat. Stir in brown sugar until well blended. Stir in egg and vanilla. Add flour mixture, stirring until just combined. Pour into prepared pan.

3 Bake for 20 to 25 minutes or until a wooden toothpick comes out clean inserted in the center. Cool on a wire rack. Top with favorite gluten-free ice cream and gluten-free topping. *Serves 8.*

Read the Label

Ice creams vary a lot from brand to brand. Most vanilla ice creams are gluten-free. Many flavored ice creams, however, are not. Be sure and read the label or call the manufacturer to be sure.

This chewy blonde brownie is delicious by itself, but try adding a dollop of whipped cream topped with chopped nuts for a special treat.

Nutrition Per Serving:
290 calories, 12g fat, 4g saturated fat, 39mg cholesterol, 44g carbohydrate, 1g fiber, 2g protein

Happy Birthday Cake **V**

Read the Label

For a special occasion it's fun to use food coloring to tint sweets. Most food colorings are gluten-free. To be safe, however, always read the label and look for words such as "emulsifiers." You also can color foods with natural colorings such as pomegranate or grape juice. But keep in mind that it's harder to control the final color with natural colorings.

6

Nutrition Per Serving:
550 calories,
13g fat, 4g
saturated fat, 5mg
cholesterol, 370mg
sodium, 108g
carbohydrate, 1g
fiber, 4g protein

Ingredients

5 egg whites

½ teaspoon cream of tartar

1½ cups sugar

½ cup butter, softened

2 cups gluten-free all-purpose flour such as Domata Living™ Flour

¾ cup milk

3½ teaspoons baking powder

1 teaspoon salt

¼ cup carbonated water

1 teaspoon almond extract

Food coloring

1 recipe Butter Frosting

Directions

1 Preheat oven to 350°F. Grease and flour a 10-inch fluted tube pan or 13x9-inch baking pan. Set aside. In a mixing bowl beat egg whites and cream of tartar with an electric mixer until mixture forms stiff peaks. See Photo A. Set aside.

2 In a large bowl beat sugar and butter until creamy. Add flour, ¼ cup of the milk, baking powder, and salt. Beat on low speed until just blended, scraping bowl constantly. Beat in remaining milk, carbonated water, and almond extract until just combined. Batter will be thick and sticky. Fold in beaten egg whites. See Photo B. Remove 1 cup of the batter and tint with food coloring. Pour plain batter into prepared pan. Top with colored batter. See Photo C. Use a skewer to mix the colored batter into the white batter. See Photo D.

3 Bake for about 45 minutes for tube pan and 35 to 40 minutes for 13x9-inch pan, or until a wooden toothpick comes out clean when inserted in center. Cool on a wire rack (cool tube cake for about 2 minutes before removing from pan). Cake will shrink from pan while cooling. Frost cake with Butter Frosting. *Serves 12.*

Butter Frosting

1 In a large mixing bowl beat ½ cup softened butter with electric mixer until fluffy. Slowly beat in 2 cups powdered sugar. Beat in ¼ cup whole milk and 1 teaspoon vanilla or almond flavoring. Slowly beat in 4 cups powdered sugar and enough milk to make spreadable consistency. If desired, tint with food coloring.

A   B   C   D

This beautiful frosted cake will make everyone sing "Happy Birthday." But just wait until the cake is cut to reveal the marbled pattern inside, and then you'll hear "oohs" and "aahs."

Double Chocolate Cookies

Read the Label

Be sure to read the label or call the company when choosing chocolate chips. One brand that is gluten-free is Nestlé® Tollhouse® Semi-Sweet Morsels. Look for words like "food starch" or "natural flavorings." These general terms may mean that there is gluten in the product.

Ingredients

1½ cups granulated sugar

1 cup butter, softened

2 eggs

2 teaspoons vanilla

2¼ cups Domata Living™ gluten-free all-purpose flour

⅔ cup unsweetened cocoa powder

¾ teaspoon baking soda

¼ teaspoon salt

1½ cups gluten-free dark or semisweet chocolate chips

½ cup walnuts, chopped (optional)

1 recipe Powdered Sugar Drizzle

Directions

1 Preheat oven to 350°F. In a large mixing bowl beat sugar and butter with an electric mixer until creamy. Beat in eggs and vanilla until light and fluffy. See Photo A.

2 In another large mixing bowl stir together flour, cocoa powder, baking soda, and salt. Stir flour mixture into butter mixture. Stir in chocolate pieces and, if desired, walnuts. See Photo B.

3 Drop by rounded tablespoon onto a greased cookie sheet and slightly flatten with your fingers. See Photo C. Bake about 10 minutes or until edges are firm. Cool slightly on cookie sheet before transferring to a wire rack to cool completely. Drizzle with Powdered Sugar Drizzle. *Serves 24.*

Powdered Sugar Drizzle

1 In a small bowl stir together 2 cups powdered sugar, 3 tablespoons milk, and 1 teaspoon vanilla until smooth. Place in a small plastic sandwich bag, cut off corner of bag, and drizzle over cookies.

Note: For tips on drizzling frostings, see page 194.

Carol says:
These cookies are chewy and delightfully chocolatey—one of my favorite recipes.

Nutrition Per Serving:
250 calories, 12g fat, 5g saturated fat, 26mg cholesterol, 88mg sodium, 35g carbohydrate, 2g fiber, 3g protein

Recipe courtesy of Domata Living™

Cocoa powder and gluten-free semisweet or dark chocolate chips combine to make these easy-to-fix drop cookies a real chocolate lover's delight.

Peanut Butter Cookies

Read the Label

Not all peanut butters will work in a gluten-free meal plan. Look for natural peanut butters in the refrigerator case at the supermarket, and always read the label before deciding on a brand.

Ingredients

½ cup butter, softened

½ cup granulated sugar

½ cup packed brown sugar

½ cup creamy or chunky gluten-free peanut butter

1 egg

½ teaspoon vanilla

1¼ cups gluten-free all-purpose flour such as Domata Living™ flour

¾ teaspoon baking soda

¼ teaspoon salt

Additional gluten-free flour

Directions

1 In a large bowl beat butter, granulated sugar, brown sugar, and peanut butter with an electric mixer until creamy. Beat in egg and vanilla until light and fluffy. Add flour, baking soda, and salt, beating until just blended. Cover and chill in refrigerator for 1 hour.

2 Preheat oven to 375°F. Using your hands, form dough into 2-inch balls. Place the balls on an ungreased cookie sheet. Dip the tines of a table fork into flour and slightly flatten each ball of dough by pressing it twice, at right angles, to form a crisscross pattern.

3 Bake for 8 to 10 minutes or until very lightly browned. Do not overbake. Cool on a wire rack or waxed paper. *Serves 12.*

Tuck these peanut-butter cookies in your lunch tote. Then you can munch them for a mid-morning snack or as an after-lunch indulgence.

Nutrition Per Serving:
346 calories, 20g fat, 7g saturated fat, 56mg cholesterol, 225mg sodium, 37g carbohydrate, 2g fiber, 8g protein

Chewy Chocolate Brownies **Ⓥ**

Ingredients

½ cup butter, melted

½ cup gluten-free semi-sweet chocolate chips

1 cup gluten-free all-purpose flour such as Domata Living™ Flour

¾ cup sugar

½ teaspoon baking soda

2 eggs, beaten

2 tablespoons carbonated water

½ teaspoon vanilla

½ cup chopped nuts

1 recipe Chocolate Frosting

Directions

1 Preheat oven to 350°F. In a small saucepan heat butter on low heat until melted. Stir in chocolate chips until melted. Remove from heat.

2 In a medium bowl mix together flour, sugar, and baking soda; Add chocolate mixture. Stir in eggs, carbonated water, and vanilla until combined. Stir in nuts. Pour into a greased 8x8-inch baking pan. Bake for 20 minutes. Cool on a wire rack. Frost with Chocolate Frosting. *Serves 12.*

Chocolate Frosting

1 In a small saucepan mix together ¾ cup sugar, 3 tablespoons butter, and 3 tablespoons milk. Bring to boiling and stir for 1 minute. Mix in ½ cup gluten-free semisweet chocolate chips and stir until melted. Cool slightly before frosting.

Freeze for Later

These brownies freeze very well even after they're frosted. Freeze them in single layers in freezer containers so the shape of the brownie stays intact.

Add a Flavor Variation

If you are a coffee fan, you'll want to add some to these decadent bars. Stir 1 tablespoon gluten-free instant coffee granules into the flour mixture before mixing the batter for a heavenly mocha flavor.

If your favorite bar cookie is the brownie, try one of these. Garnish with more chopped nuts and a bit of powdered sugar.

Nutrition Per Serving:
255 calories, 14g fat, 5g saturated fat, 44mg cholesterol, 166mg sodium, 30g carbohydrate, 2g fiber, 3g protein

Lemon-Filled Cupcakes V

Plan Ahead and Save Time

These sweet little cakes are just the thing for a party because you can do most of the work ahead. Make the cupcakes and freeze them for up to 2 months. Then on party day, fill the cupcakes and bake on the meringue topper.

Ingredients

1 cup sugar
½ cup butter, softened
2 eggs
2 teaspoons vanilla
1½ cups gluten-free all-purpose flour such as Domata Living™ Flour
1½ teaspoons baking powder
½ cup milk
1 recipe Meringue Topping
1½ cups gluten-free lemon curd such as Dickinson's® Lemon Curd

Directions

1 Preheat oven to 350°F. Grease 12 muffin cups. Set aside. In a large mixing bowl beat sugar and butter with an electric mixer until creamy. Beat in eggs and vanilla.

2 In a small bowl combine flour and baking powder. Alternately add flour mixture and milk to egg mixture, beating until combined. Filled prepared muffin cups three-fourths full. Bake for 15 minutes. Remove from cups; cool on a wire rack.

3 Prepare Meringue Topping. Using a long serrated knife, cut cupcakes in half horizontally. See Photo A. Spread lemon curd on the bottom halves of cupcakes. See Photo B. Replace top halves.

4 Spread meringue on tops of filled cupcakes, swirling mixture to make peaks. Place cupcakes on baking sheet. Bake about 15 minutes more or until meringue is lightly browned. *Serves 12.*

Meringue Topping

1 In a medium mixing bowl combine 4 egg whites, 1 teaspoon vanilla, and ½ teaspoon cream of tartar.

2 Beat with electric mixer on high speed until mixture just begins to form soft peaks. Slowly add ½ cup sugar, beating on high speed about 5 minutes or until mixture forms stiff, glossy peaks.

Note: For step-by-step photos for preparing meringue, see page 193.

Elizabeth says:

Unlike a streusel topping or a pie crust, a meringue topping contains no gluten. It adds a spectacular finish to this memorable dessert.

Nutrition Per Serving:

270 calories, 9g fat, 3g saturated fat, 44mg cholesterol, 122mg sodium, 44g carbohydrate, 1g fiber, 4g protein

6

A   B   C

Gluten-free lemon curd gives these simply elegant desserts a captivating citrus flavor. Look for it in the jelly aisle of the supermarket.

Chocolate Cake ⓥ

Freeze for Later

You'll never be at a loss for what to serve for dessert if you keep layers of this cake on hand in the freezer. Bake the cake layers, cool them completely, and wrap each layer individually in plastic wrap. Place each layer in a resealable freezer bag and freeze for up to 2 months. To serve, thaw the layers completely and frost.

Ingredients

- 2 cups + 2 tablespoons Domata Living™ gluten-free all-purpose flour
- 2 cups sugar
- ¾ cup unsweetened cocoa powder
- 2 teaspoons baking powder
- 1 teaspoon salt
- ½ teaspoon baking soda
- 1¼ cups water
- 4 large eggs
- ¾ cup canola oil
- 2 teaspoons vanilla
- 1 recipe Creamy Chocolate Frosting
- Fresh raspberries (optional)
- Fresh mint sprigs (optional)

Directions

1 Preheat oven to 350°F. Generously grease two 8-inch round cake pans. For each pan, cut a piece of waxed paper slightly larger than the pan. See Photo A. Fold the paper in half, in half again, and in half again. See Photo B. Fold the paper again and place the point in the center of the pan. Trim the paper to fit the pan. See Photo C. Open up the paper and place in bottom of pan. See Photo D.

2 In a large mixing bowl stir together flour, sugar, cocoa powder, baking powder, salt, and baking soda. Add water, eggs, oil, and vanilla. Beat with an electric mixer on low speed until just blended, scraping side of bowl as needed. Pour batter into prepared pans.

3 Bake about 35 minutes or until a wooden toothpick comes out clean when inserted in the centers. Cool cake layers in pans for 15 minutes. Turn out onto wire racks, carefully remove paper, and cool completely. Fill and frost cake with Creamy Chocolate Frosting. If desired, garnish with raspberries and mint. *Serves 12.*

Creamy Chocolate Frosting

1 In a medium saucepan stir together 1½ cups sugar, 6 tablespoons butter, 6 tablespoons milk, and 2 tablespoons light-color corn syrup.

2 Cover and bring to boiling over medium-high heat. Remove lid and boil for 2 minutes, stirring constantly. Remove from heat. Stir in 1 cup gluten-free semisweet chocolate chips until melted.

Note: When making a 2-layer cake that is gluten-free, it is important to prepare the pans as directed so the cake layers do not stick.

Nutrition Per Serving:
650 calories, 27g fat, 7g saturated fat, 81mg cholesterol, 428mg sodium, 101g carbohydrate, 3g fiber, 6g protein

Recipe courtesy of Domata Living™

A B C

Cocoa powder and gluten-free flour team up with remarkable results in this rich, moist, and delightfully dense cake. Even the most difficult to please will proclaim it "spectacular."

Cashew-Coconut Brittle Ⓥ EF

Add a Flavor Variation

Like almonds better than cashews? Any nut will work in this recipe. Simply substitute the nut that you like for the cashews. Try almonds, pecans, or even the conventional peanut—they are all delicious.

This is no ordinary brittle. Bite into a piece and the amazing flavors of cashews and coconut will tantalize your taste buds.

Nutrition Per Serving:
240 calories, 9g fat, 3g saturated fat, 1mg cholesterol, 292mg sodium, 40g carbohydrate, 1g fiber, 2g protein

Ingredients

2 cups sugar
1 cup light-color corn syrup
½ cup water
½ teaspoon salt
2 tablespoons butter
2 cups cashews
2 teaspoons baking soda
1 teaspoon vanilla
1 cup shredded coconut

Directions

1 Preheat oven to 200°F. Generously grease two baking sheets with butter. Place in oven, then turn off oven, keeping baking sheets warm.

2 In a large heavy saucepan combine sugar, corn syrup, water, and salt. Bring mixture to boiling; add butter. Clip a candy thermometer to side of pan. Cook, stirring frequently, until mixture reaches 250°F. Stir in cashews.

3 Cook, stirring constantly, until mixture reaches 305°F. Remove pan from heat; remove thermometer. Quickly stir in baking soda and vanilla. Stir in coconut.

4 Spread mixture in a thin layer on each warm baking sheet. Cool. Break into bite-size pieces. *Serves 20.*

Cranberry-Pecan Toffee Ⓥ ⓔ

Ingredients

¾ cup dried cranberries

1 cup butter

1 cup sugar

3 tablespoons water

1 tablespoon light-color corn syrup

1 teaspoon vanilla

¾ cup chopped pecans

½ cup gluten-free chocolate chips

¼ cup finely chopped pecans

Directions

1 Grease an 8x8-inch baking pan with butter; sprinkle the bottom with dried cranberries. Set aside.

2 In a large heavy saucepan heat the 1 cup butter until melted. Stir in sugar, water, corn syrup, and vanilla until combined. Clip a candy thermometer to side of pan. Cook over medium to high heat until mixture boils and reaches 300°F. Remove from heat; remove thermometer. Quickly stir in chopped pecans.

3 Spread mixture evenly in prepared pan. Sprinkle with half of the chocolate chips. Let stand until chocolate melts; spread over candy. Sprinkle with half of the finely chopped pecans. Cool. Turn candy over and repeat with remaining chocolate pieces and remaining finely chopped pecans. Cool. Break into bite-size pieces. *Serves 20.*

Add a Flavor Variation

Make this toffee truly your own by varying the dried fruit and chocolate you use. You can substitute snipped dried cherries or dried apricots, dried currants, or golden raisins for the cranberries. And take your choice of milk, semisweet, or dark chocolate chips.

If toffee is your weakness, you'll love this dressed-up version. The cranberries add a fresh-tasting hint of tartness and a festive bit of red color, making the candy perfect for the holidays.

Nutrition Per Serving:
200 calories, 14g fat, 4g saturated fat, 11mg cholesterol, 8mg sodium, 19g carbohydrate, 1g fiber, 1g protein

Homemade Marshmallows Ⓥ ⓁⒻ ⒸⒻ ⒺⒻ

Read the Label

There are many marshmallows on the market that are gluten-free. However, there are just as many brands that do contain gluten. So making your own marshmallows will guarantee this sweet treat is gluten-free.

Ingredients

2 tablespoons unflavored gelatin such as Knox®

¼ cup cold water

1 teaspoon clear vanilla

½ teaspoon salt

2 cups granulated sugar

¼ cup water

Food coloring (optional)

Powdered sugar

Directions

1 Grease an 8x8-inch glass baking dish with butter. Set aside. In a large mixing bowl sprinkle gelatin over ¼ cup cold water to dissolve. See Photo A. Stir in vanilla and salt. Set aside.

2 In a medium saucepan combine sugar and ¼ cup water. Bring mixture to boiling. Clip a candy thermometer to side of pan. Cook, stirring frequently, until mixture reaches 238°F. Remove from heat; remove thermometer. Slowly pour syrup over gelatin mixture while beating on medium speed with electric mixer. See Photo B.

3 Continue to beat with an electric mixer on high speed until very thick and white. See Photo C. If desired, tint with food coloring. Pour into prepared pan, pushing mixture to edges. See Photo D.

4 Dust with powdered sugar. Cover and let stand overnight. Cut into squares. If desired, dust again with powdered sugar. *Serves 16.*

Carol says:

Not only are these marshmallows sweet and pretty, they're also fun to make. Beating the sugar syrup into the gelatin gives them their magical texture.

6

Nutrition Per Serving:
105 calories, 0g fat, 0g saturated fat, 0mg cholesterol, 74mg sodium, 26g carbohydrate, 0g fiber, 1g protein

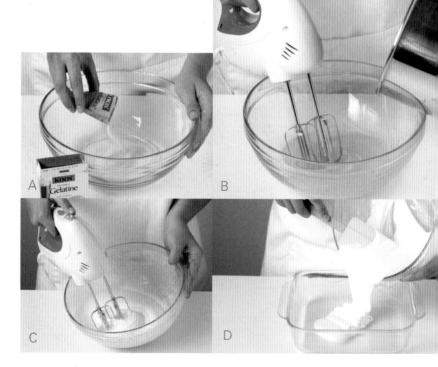

If you've never had a homemade marshmallow,
make this recipe and discover how soft, sweet,
and special they are. Tint them any color you like
or leave them creamy white.

Cookies, cakes, and candies are treats that no one wants to do without. Candies are relatively easy to make gluten-free because gluten is not a typical ingredient. However, making gluten-free cookies and cakes can be challenging. Cakes made with eggs are the best to try, because these cakes are based on eggs, not gluten, for structure. Cakes that are based on an egg white foam, such as angel food cakes, sponge cakes, and chiffon cakes are especially easy to make gluten-free. Cookies do not require as much "lift" and therefore are a bit easier to make than cakes. Although, gluten-free cookies often spread out too thinly around the edges and can easily burn. So try these tips to help make your favorite baked goods a gluten-free success:

- In the beginning of a cake or cookie recipe, creaming the sugar and butter can add more air into the recipe. Start with room temperature butter and cream with sugar for several minutes or until very fluffy.

- When placing cookie dough on the cookie sheet, use a scoop for identically-sized cookies to ensure even baking. Placing the cookies on parchment paper will make them easier to remove from the pan. Halfway through the cooking time, turn the pan 180 degrees in the oven to ensure even cooking.

- Adding an egg white foam to a cake recipe adds air and lightness. Try beating one egg white into a foam and folding it into the cake batter. Depending on the specific cake, this may help with the final result.

Carol says:
Using gluten-free flour in cakes that are meant to be light and fluffy may require adding a bit of carbonated water to get the proper texture. Oftentimes that means that the cake may fall a bit after taking it out of the oven but it will still be lighter than without the additional carbonated liquid.

7 Snacks, Appetizers, and Drinks

Snack Mix ⓥ ⒺⒻ ⓌⒼ

Add a Flavor Variation

This snack mix can include any of your favorite dried fruits or nuts. Try dried mango or sunflower seeds for a different taste combination.

Ingredients

- 2 cups Rice Chex®
- 2 cups Corn Chex®
- 2 cups gluten-free cereal such as Gorilla Munch®
- ½ cup whole cashews
- ½ cup whole almonds
- ½ cup raisins
- ½ cup chopped dried apricots
- ½ cup butter, melted
- ½ cup sugar
- 1 teaspoon ground cinnamon

Directions

1 Preheat oven to 250°F. In a large bowl combine cereals, cashews, almonds, raisins, and dried apricots. Pour melted butter over mixture and toss lightly. Mix sugar and cinnamon and sprinkle over cereal mixture. Mix well.

2 Pour into a large shallow baking pan. Bake for 1 hour, stirring every 15 minutes. Cool. *Serves 20.*

Carol says:
We used Rice Chex® and Corn Chex® as the main ingredients when developing this recipe. They are inexpensive and guaranteed gluten-free.

A wonderful blend of flavors and textures makes this snack mix a great addition to any party.

Nutrition Per Serving:
190 calories, 10g fat, 2g saturated fat, 6mg cholesterol, 131mg sodium, 24g carbohydrate, 2g fiber, 3g protein

Mango-Peach Smoothie Ⓥ ⓁⒻ ⒽⓅ ⒺⒻ

Ingredients

2 bananas

2 peaches

1 mango

1 cup gluten-free plain yogurt

1 teaspoon sugar

1 teaspoon ground cinnamon

10 ice cubes

Directions

1 Peel and slice bananas; peel, pit, and chop peaches and mango. Place fruit in a blender. Add yogurt, sugar, and cinnamon.

2 Cover and blend on low speed until combined. Add ice cubes. Cover and blend on high speed until well mixed. Serve cold. *Serves 2.*

Add a Flavor Variation
This creamy sipper is delicious with a number of different fruits. Try strawberries or blueberries in place of the peaches and mango. Keep the bananas though—they add body and help create smooth texture.

Everyone loves fruit drinks. This one mixes bananas, peaches, and mango with gluten-free yogurt for a healthy snack.

Nutrition Per Serving:
320 calories, 3g fat, 1g saturated fat, 7mg cholesterol, 89mg sodium, 71g carbohydrate, 8g fiber, 10g protein

Add a Flavor Variation

If you like, add another topping to these easy-to-make snacks. Chopped fresh spinach, sliced black or green olives, or a little drained crushed pineapple are all great additions.

Mini Pizzas **LF** **WG**

Ingredients

¾ cup brown rice flour
¾ cup tapioca flour
¾ cup cornmeal
2 tablespoons sugar
½ teaspoon baking powder
½ teaspoon salt
1 egg
¼ cup water
2 tablespoons olive oil
¾ cup gluten-free pizza sauce such as Dei Frateilli®Pizza Sauce
½ cup gluten-free miniature pepperoni slices such as Hormel®
1½ cups finely shredded mozzarella or Italian blend cheese

Directions

1 Preheat oven to 375°F. In a small bowl mix rice flour, tapioca flour, cornmeal, sugar, baking powder, and salt.

2 In another small bowl beat together egg, water, and oil. Add egg mixture to flour mixture and mix well. Add more water if necessary to form a ball.

3 Divide dough into 12 pieces; form into balls and place in shallow baking pans. Using your fingers, press each ball of dough into a round flat shape. See Photo A.

4 Spread each crust with 1 tablespoon of the pizza sauce. See Photo B. Top with pepperoni. Sprinkle each with 2 tablespoons of the cheese. See Photo C.

5 Bake for 10 minutes. Increase oven temperature to 400°F. Bake about 10 minutes more or until crust begins to brown and cheese is melted and brown. *Serves 12.*

7

Carol says:
I have these ready to bake in the freezer so when Marcia and her family stop by unexpectedly I can just pop them in the oven.

Nutrition Per Serving:
180 calories, 4g fat, 1g saturated fat, 23mg cholesterol, 300mg sodium, 28g carbohydrate, 2g fiber, 8g protein

A   B   C

Make plenty of these little pizza snacks
because they go fast! If you like, personalize
the toppings so each person can have a mini
pizza that's made-to-order.

Spicy Hummus ⓋⓁⒻⒸⒻⒺⒻ

Add a Flavor Variation

Hummus is fun to make because it can be flavored in so many different ways. Try onion powder, dried basil, dried oregano, chopped fresh dill, or lemon pepper in place of the jalapeño pepper. Or stir in some chopped gluten-free black olives, sliced green onion, or chopped fresh tomato.

Ingredients

2 cups canned garbanzo beans, rinsed and drained

2 cloves garlic, finely minced

1 teaspoon minced jalapeño pepper

½ teaspoon salt

½ teaspoon black pepper

3 tablespoons lemon juice

3 tablespoons tahini (sesame paste)

3 tablespoons olive oil

½ to 1 cup tomato juice

Chopped gluten-free black olives (optional)

Coarsely chopped tomato (optional)

Directions

1 Place garbanzo beans in a food processor. Cover and process until blended. See Photo A.

2 Add garlic, jalapeño pepper, salt, and black pepper. Cover and process until combined. See Photo B. Add lemon juice, tahini, and olive oil. Cover and process until well blended. Mixture will be thick.

3 With machine running, slowly add enough tomato juice to make mixture the desired consistency. See Photo C. Transfer to a serving bowl. If desired, garnish with olives and tomato. *Serves 10.*

Note: Garlic must be finely minced for uniform flavor.

> **Elizabeth says:**
> The unique texture of hummus comes from the natural starchiness of the garbanzo bean when it's processed with tahini, olive oil, and tomato juice.

Nutrition Per Serving:
125 calories, 7g fat,
1g saturated fat,
0mg cholesterol,
418mg sodium,
13g fiber, 3g fiber,
3g protein

A   B   C

Gluten-free Tuscan Flatbread (see page 96) or Crispy Crackers (see page 144) are the perfect partners for this zesty sesame-flavored garbanzo bean spread.

Crispy Crackers Ⓥ ⒧Ⓕ ⓌⒼ

Add a Flavor Variation

For a creative twist, add an herb such as basil, thyme, rosemary, or oregano to the dry ingredients before making these crackers. One teaspoon is just right for most herbs, but because rosemary is a bit stronger, use only ½ teaspoon.

Ingredients

1   cup rice flour
⅔ cup cornmeal
¼ cup millet flour
¼ cup tapioca flour
1   teaspoon salt
¾ cup water
1   egg, beaten
1¼ teaspoons olive oil
2   tablespoons butter, melted
Additional salt

Directions

1 In a large mixing bowl combine rice flour, cornmeal, millet flour, tapioca flour, and salt. Make a well in the dry ingredients. Add water, egg, and oil and stir until just mixed. Dough will be soft. Cover and chill for several hours or until easy to roll out.

2 Preheat oven to 375°F. Lightly grease a baking sheet. Set aside. On a lightly floured surface, roll out dough to ¼-inch thickness. Cut into about 24 crackers. Using a fork, prick the tops of crackers. Place 1 inch apart on prepared baking sheet. Drizzle with melted butter and pinch of salt if desired.

3 Bake for 20 to 25 minutes or until golden brown. Cool on wire racks. Makes about 24 crackers. *Serves 12.*

7

Cornmeal adds delightful crunch to these buttery crackers. They're terrific for parties or to go with soup.

Nutrition Per Serving:
110 calories, 3g fat, 1g saturated fat, 20mg cholesterol, 200mg sodium, 18g carbohydrate, 1g fiber, 2g protein

Lettuce Wraps (LF) (CF) (EF)

Ingredients

8 large lettuce leaves

1 tablespoon olive oil

¼ cup chopped green onion

¼ cup finely chopped celery

3 cups chopped uncooked chicken

1 8-ounce can water chestnuts, drained and chopped

1 tablespoon gluten-free soy sauce

2 teaspoons minced fresh ginger

Directions

1 Wash lettuce leaves and pat dry. Set aside.

2 In a medium skillet heat oil on medium heat. Add onion and celery; cook and stir until tender. Add chicken. Cook, stirring frequently, about 6 minutes or until chicken is no longer pink and fully cooked. Stir in water chestnuts, soy sauce, and ginger.

3 To serve, spoon chicken mixture onto lettuce leaves. Serve wrapped or unwrapped. *Serves 8.*

Plan Ahead and Save Time

Because you'll want to cook the filling for these appetizer wraps at the last minute, it's helpful to do some of the prep work ahead. Cut up the chicken, onion, celery, and water chestnuts and store them in separate containers in the refrigerator so they're ready to go when it's time to cook and serve.

These elegant wraps make a fabulous first course for a party menu. The Asian-seasoned chicken filling starts the meal off with a flavor bang.

Nutrition Per Serving:
41 calories, 2g fat, 0g saturated fat, 13mg cholesterol, 145mg sodium, 0g carbohydrate, 0g fiber, 5g protein

Cheese Quesadillas Ⓥ 🄻🄵 🄴🄵 🆆🄶

The Cost

Quesadillas are inexpensive to make and serve. One quesadilla costs about 40¢ and serves three.

Add a Flavor Variation

For a change of pace, tuck some sliced olives or chopped avocado into these cheddar-filled quesadillas.

Ingredients

1½ cups shredded cheddar cheese

¼ cup chopped red sweet pepper

¼ cup chopped green sweet pepper

¼ cup chopped jalapeño peppers

1 tablespoon olive oil

6 corn tortillas

½ cup gluten-free salsa such as Pace® Picante Salsa

Directions

1 In a small bowl combine cheese, sweet peppers, and jalapeño peppers. Set aside.

2 In a large skillet heat oil on medium heat. Place one tortilla in pan. Spoon one-third of the cheese mixture onto tortilla. See Photo A.

3 Place another tortilla on top of cheese mixture. Press lightly. See Photo B.

4 Cook until cheese is melted and tortillas are brown and crispy, turning with a spatula to cook both sides. See Photo C. Remove from skillet. Make two more quesadillas. Cut quesadillas into wedges. Serve with salsa. *Serves 9.*

> Marcia says:
> We make these quesadillas all the time at our house—both as appetizers for a party and as a spur-of-the-moment treat.

7

Nutrition Per Serving:

135 calories, 8g fat, 5g saturated fat, 23mg cholesterol, 230mg sodium, 9g carbohydrate, 1g fiber, 7g protein

A   B   C

So simple to make and naturally gluten-free, these little wedges will satisfy everyone at your parties. Or turn them into a meal by adding some shredded cooked chicken or cubed gluten-free ham. Serve fresh fruit as a side dish.

Chocolate Shake Ⓥ ⓗⓟ ⓔⓕ

Read the Label

Did you know that the malt in malted milk shakes contains gluten? True malt powder is made from barley. The process for producing the powder involves allowing the barley to sprout and then drying and finely grinding the sprouted barley. Because barley is an offending grain to those with gluten intolerance, you'll want to skip malted shakes.

Enjoy a soda fountain treat at home by whirling together this quick-fixing shake.

Nutrition Per Serving:
800 calories, 33g fat, 20g saturated fat, 125mg cholesterol, 243mg sodium, 121g carbohydrate, 5g fiber, 13g protein

Ingredients

¼ cup sugar

¼ cup unsweetened cocoa powder

½ cup water

1 quart vanilla ice cream

½ cup whole milk

Gluten-free chocolate curls (optional)

Directions

1 In a small saucepan mix sugar and cocoa powder. Add water and mix well. Bring to boiling and cook for 1 minute. Remove from heat; cool slightly.

2 In a blender combine ice cream and milk. Cover and blend until smooth. Add cocoa mixture. Cover and blend until well mixed.

3 If desired, garnish each serving with chocolate curls. Serve immediately. *Serves 2.*

Tempura Shrimp CF

Ingredients

1 egg

¼ cup rice flour

¼ cup tapioca flour

¼ teaspoon salt

½ cup carbonated water

Oil for frying

8 large or 12 medium shrimp, peeled and deveined

Gluten-free cocktail sauce (optional)

Directions

1 In a small bowl beat egg. Set aside. In a medium bowl mix rice flour, tapioca flour, and salt. Add carbonated water and mix well. Mixture should resemble very thick cream. Add more carbonated water if necessary to reach proper thickness.

2 In a large skillet heat oil on medium to medium-high heat to 375°F. Dip shrimp into egg, then into flour mixture. Cook in hot oil about 6 minutes or until shrimp are cooked and coating is golden brown, turning to cook both sides. If desired, serve with cocktail sauce. *Serves 4.*

Plan Ahead and Save Time
You can peel and devein the shrimp several hours before you're ready to cook them. Just keep the shrimp well chilled on ice in the refrigerator until you are ready to prepare the meal.

The light coating for this gluten-free tempura allows the delicate flavor of the shrimp to come through.

Nutrition Per Serving:
136 calories, 10g fat, 0g saturated fat, 74mg cholesterol, 196mg sodium, 16g carbohydrate, 0g fiber, 6g protein

Gluten-free snacking can be tricky

because many processed snack foods contain gluten. But you can still fulfill those between-meal cravings with a little foresight and smart choices. If you are travelling or on the go, fill a sandwich bag with the following gluten-free snacks and toss it in your purse or briefcase when you head out the door:

- Nuts, seeds, or peanuts
- Raisins, dates, or other dried fruit
- Popcorn
- Apples, bananas, or other fresh fruit that travels well
- Carrots, broccoli, or other crunchy vegetables that won't soften quickly
- Original flavor potato and tortilla chips—usually gluten-free

> **Marcia says:**
> It pays to plan ahead and pack a gluten-free snack (or two or three!) when travelling or heading out for the day. You'll appreciate your effort once you are on the road.

Snacking at home offers you more options because the fridge is nearby. Try to remember to have these gluten-free snacks on hand:

- Gluten-free yogurt—most are gluten-free.
- Gluten-free cheese—all non-processed cheeses are gluten-free.
- Vanilla ice cream—many other flavors are gluten-free as well.
- Gluten-free pickles
- Hard-boiled eggs
- Salsa or hummus for dips—most are gluten-free.

8 Desserts and Pies

Key Lime Mousse ⓥ ⒧ⓕ ⒠ⓕ

Add a Flavor Variation

For tropical flavor, add ½ cup shredded coconut to this dessert. Simply fold in the coconut with the whipped topping. If you like, toast a little coconut to sprinkle on top in place of the shaved chocolate.

Ingredients

1 3-ounce package lime gelatin such as Jell-O®

⅓ cup boiling water

1 cup plain yogurt

1 6-ounce carton gluten-free key lime yogurt

1 8-ounce carton gluten-free whipped topping such as Cool Whip®

Shaved chocolate (optional)

Directions

1 Pour gelatin into a large bowl. Add boiling water and stir until gelatin is dissolved. See Photo A.

2 Add plain yogurt and key lime yogurt and mix well. See Photo B.

3 Fold in whipped topping. See Photo C. Spoon into dessert dishes. See Photo D. If desired, sprinkle with chocolate. Chill until set. *Serves 8.*

Carol says:

You can make this dessert with other flavors of yogurt and gelatin. Try using peach yogurt with peach gelatin or strawberry yogurt with strawberry gelatin.

Nutrition Per Serving:

189 calories, 5g fat, 4g saturated fat, 3mg cholesterol, 141 mg sodium, 30g carbohydrate, 0g fiber, 6g protein

A

B

C

D

This rich, smooth dessert can be dressed up for a party or down for a casual treat. For an everyday family meal, spoon it into custard cups instead of crystal glasses. No matter how you serve this easy mousse, everyone will love it!

Read the Label
Tapioca is a natural thickening agent used in many pudding, stew, and sauce recipes. Gluten-free, it is a good substitute for wheat flour when it comes to thickening. Tapioca comes from the root of a shrub-like plant called cassava, which is native to South America. By itself, tapioca is nearly flavorless and contributes little nutritional value.

Naturally gluten-free, this simple tapioca pudding is a delicious way to end a meal.

Nutrition Per Serving:
141 calories, 1g fat, 0g saturated fat, 38mg cholesterol, 63 mg sodium, 2g carbohydrate, 0g fiber, 5g protein

Tapioca Pudding **V** **LF**

Ingredients

½ cup sugar
¼ cup quick-cooking tapioca
3 cups milk
1 egg, beaten
1 teaspoon vanilla
Fresh fruit (optional)
Chocolate curls (optional)

Directions

1 In a medium saucepan mix sugar and tapioca. In a medium bowl mix together milk and egg. Stir milk mixture into sugar mixture. Let stand for 10 minutes.

2 Bring to boiling. Boil about 2 minutes or until thick, stirring constantly. Remove from heat. Stir in vanilla. Serve warm or cold. If desired, serve with fruit and garnish with chocolate. *Serves 6.*

> **Marcia says:**
> I serve this easy-to-make dessert with fruits that the kids love. Strawberries, bananas, and peaches are their favorites.

Apple Crisp Ⓥ ⓛⒻ ⒺⒻ

Ingredients

4 cups peeled and sliced
   tart apples such as
   Granny Smith
1 cup granulated sugar
2 tablespoons tapioca
   flour
½ cup packed brown
   sugar
¼ cup brown rice flour
¼ cup butter

Directions

1 Preheat oven to 350°F. Lightly grease a 2-quart
shallow baking dish. Layer apples in prepared dish.
In a small bowl mix granulated sugar and tapioca
flour. Sprinkle over apples; toss lightly.

2 In a small bowl mix brown sugar, brown rice flour,
and butter until crumbly. Sprinkle over apples. Bake
about 40 minutes or until bubbly. *Serves 6.*

Carol says:
Because apples contain pectin, a
natural thickener, we found that a little
rice flour is all it takes to make this
apple dessert the perfect texture.

**Add a Flavor
Variation**
*Add texture and
crunch to this
crisp by
stirring
raisins or
chopped
walnuts into
the apple mixture
before sprinkling on
the topping.*

Sweet brown sugar
combines with
tart Granny Smith
apples to create a
sensational apple
crisp. Serve it with a
scoop of ice cream
for a real treat.

**Nutrition
Per Serving:**
337 calories, 8g
fat, 5g saturated
fat, 20mg
cholesterol,
9mg sodium,
68g carbohydrate,
1g fiber, 1g protein

Rice Pudding Ⓥ ⓛⓕ ⒽⓅ

8

Add a Flavor Variation

Boost the flavor and texture of this creamy dessert by including chopped nuts. Choose pecans, walnuts, or hazelnuts. Add ½ cup when you mix in the rice mixture. Then sprinkle a few on top as you spoon on the brown sugar.

Ingredients

5 eggs

2 cups whole milk

¾ cup packed brown sugar

1 teaspoon ground cinnamon

1 teaspoon vanilla

½ teaspoon salt

4 cups cooked rice

¾ cup golden raisins

¾ cup dried cranberries

6 tablespoons packed brown sugar

Directions

1 Preheat oven to 325°F. Grease six 1-cup ramekins or an 8x8-inch baking pan. Set aside.

2 In a large bowl slightly beat eggs until blended. See Photo A. Add milk, ¾ cup brown sugar, cinnamon, vanilla, and salt. Mix well.

3 In another large bowl mix cooked rice, raisins, and dried cranberries. Add to egg mixture and mix well. See Photo B. Pour into prepared ramekins or pan. If using ramekins, place in a shallow baking pan.

4 Bake for about 15 minutes for ramekins or about 35 minutes for 8x8-inch pan, or until mixture is set with no liquid remaining. Remove from oven and sprinkle with 6 tablespoons brown sugar. See Photo C.

5 Set oven temperature to broil on low-heat setting. Place ramekins or pan under broiler. Broil for 45 to 60 seconds or just until sugar melts and bubbles. Watch closely to avoid burning. Remove from oven. Serve warm or cold. *Serves 6.*

Nutrition Per Serving:

463 calories, 7g fat, 3g saturated fat, 184mg cholesterol, 296 mg sodium, 91g carbohydrate, 2g fiber, 11g protein

Elizabeth says:

You can use white or brown rice in this recipe. Brown rice is more nutritious because it is a whole grain and contains more fiber and B vitamins.

A

B

C

Broiling this pudding with the sweet brown sugar topping gives it a crunchy glaze that makes it seem like a cousin to crème brûlée.

Cookie Crunch Cheesecake **Ⓥ**

Where to Find It

There are many gluten-free cookies, crackers, breads, and other gluten-free items on the market. Look in the health food section of the store or online for specific products. The flavor and texture of the different brands vary a great deal. To be sure of great taste and to save money, discover the ones you like best and keep an extra supply in the freezer to use in all kinds of cooking.

Ingredients

6   purchased gluten-free chocolate cookies or Double Chocolate Cookies (see page 124)
4   8-ounce packages cream cheese, softened
1⅓ cups sugar
2   tablespoons cornstarch
1   teaspoon vanilla
4   eggs
⅓   cup milk
1   recipe Chocolate Sauce

Directions

1 Preheat oven to 375°F. Generously grease a 9-inch springform pan. To crush cookies, place cookies in a plastic bag. Use a rolling pin to crush cookies. See Photo A. Sprinkle half of the crushed cookies in bottom of prepared pan. See Photo B.

2 In a large bowl beat cream cheese, sugar, cornstarch, and vanilla with an electric mixer until combined. See Photo C. Add eggs and milk. See Photo D. Beat for 3 minutes. Carefully pour into prepared pan. See Photo E. Sprinkle with remaining crushed cookies.

3 Bake about 40 minutes or until a 2½-inch area around the outside edge appears set when gently shaken. Cool on a wire rack for 45 minutes. Remove side of pan; cool cheesecake completely. Cover and chill for at least 4 hours before serving. Serve with warm Chocolate Sauce. *Serves 10.*

Chocolate Sauce

1 In a saucepan heat ¾ cup gluten-free semisweet chocolate chips, ¾ cup half-and-half, ¼ cup sugar, 1 tablespoon light corn syrup, and 1 tablespoon butter. Bring to boiling and boil one minute. Remove from heat and beat until smooth.

8

Nutrition Per Serving:
447 calories, 33g fat, 18g saturated fat, 183mg cholesterol, 319mg sodium, 32g carbohydrate, 0g fiber, 8g protein

A

B

C

D

It's hard to believe a cheesecake this rich and decadent can be gluten-free. Don't hesitate to serve it at parties and other special meals. It will delight and impress everyone.

Cherry-Rice Dessert 🅥 🅔🅕

Add a Flavor Variation

You can omit the cherries and add chopped dried apricots to the rice mixture. Then top the sliced dessert with an apricot glaze or thinly sliced fresh apricots.

Ingredients

1 envelope unflavored gelatin such as Knox®

3 tablespoons cold water

½ cup boiling water

2 cups whipping cream

1 cup powdered sugar

1 cup cooked white rice

1 cup crushed pineapple, drained

½ cup dried cherries

¼ cup coconut

1 teaspoon vanilla

1 recipe Cherry Sauce

Directions

1 In a small bowl sprinkle gelatin over cold water to dissolve. Stir in boiling water. Set aside.

2 In a mixing bowl beat whipping cream with an electric mixer on high speed until thick. Slowly stir in powdered sugar and gelatin mixture. Fold in rice, pineapple, cherries, coconut, and vanilla.

3 Press into a 9x5-inch loaf pan. Cover and chill for at least 4 hours or overnight. Cut into slices and serve with Cherry Sauce. *Serves 10.*

Cherry Sauce

1 In a medium saucepan combine 1 cup sugar and 1 tablespoon quick-cooking tapioca. Stir in one 14.5-ounce can pitted tart red cherries. Bring to boiling. Boil until thick, stirring constantly, about 3 minutes. Remove from heat; cool. Chill until ready to serve.

For a spectacular look, serve this fruity rice dessert with pineapple slices and sprinkle it with coconut.

Nutrition Per Serving:

375 calories, 19g fat, 12g saturated fat, 65mg cholesterol, 29mg sodium, 52g carbohydrate, 1g fiber, 2g protein

Candy Bar Dessert Ⓥ ⒺⒻ

Ingredients

1 6-ounce carton gluten-free lemon flavored yogurt

1 cup gluten-free whipped topping such as Cool Whip®

4 Granny Smith apples

3 2-ounce gluten-free chocolate-coated candy bars such as Snickers®

Directions

1 In a large bowl fold together the yogurt and whipped topping. Set aside.

2 Core and cut apples into bite-size pieces. Cut candy bars into bite-size pieces. Stir apple and candy pieces into yogurt mixture. *Serves 6.*

Marcia says:
There's no fighting over the last candy bar when we cut it up and add it to this apple dessert—everyone loves it!

Read the Label
Be careful when purchasing candy bars and other candy, because many brands contain gluten. Always check the label to be sure it is gluten-free or call the manufacturer.

In the mood for dessert, but don't want to go to a lot of fuss? Try this easy treat. It combines yogurt, apples, and sweet candy bars.

Nutrition Per Serving:
269 calories, 10g fat, 5g saturated fat, 5mg cholesterol, 101g sodium, 44g carbohydrate, 4g fiber, 4g protein

Pumpkin Custard Ⓥ ⓁⒻ

Special Health Benefits

Pumpkin's beautiful orange color lets you know it's loaded with an important antioxidant, beta-carotene. Beta-carotene is one of the plant carotenoids that is converted to vitamin A in the body. Besides being high in vitamin A, pumpkin is also a great source of potassium and fiber.

Ingredients

2 large eggs
½ cup sugar
¾ teaspoon ground cinnamon
¾ teaspoon ground ginger
¼ teaspoon salt
1 15-ounce can pumpkin
1 5-ounce can fat-free evaporated milk
Whipped cream
Ground cinnamon
1 recipe Crystallized Ginger

Directions

1 Preheat oven to 350°F. Lightly grease eight 1-cup ramekins. Set aside. In a large bowl combine eggs, sugar, ¾ teaspoon cinnamon, ground ginger, and salt. Stir in pumpkin and evaporated milk.

2 Pour into the prepared ramekins. Bake for 15 to 20 minutes or until centers are set. Remove from oven and cool on a wire rack. Top with whipped cream and more cinnamon. Garnish with Crystallized Ginger. *Serves 8.*

Crystallized Ginger

1 Peel fresh ginger using a vegetable peeler or knife. See Photo A. Cut into thin strips. See Photo B.

2 In a medium saucepan combine 3 cups water, 1 cup sugar, and 1 cup thinly sliced, peeled fresh ginger. Bring to boiling; reduce heat. Simmer, covered, for 5 minutes. Remove from heat and let stand for 20 minutes.

3 Preheat oven to 200°F. Remove ginger pieces from liquid and place on a foil-lined baking sheet. See Photo C. Bake about 15 minutes or until ginger is almost dry but still chewy. Remove from oven. Toss ginger in more sugar to coat; See Photo D. cool. Store in airtight container in freezer for up to 2 months.

8

Nutrition Per Serving:
100 calories, 1g fat, 0g saturated fat, 54mg cholesterol, 116 mg sodium, 19g carbohydrate, 2g fiber, 4g protein

Carol says:

When I have a little extra time, I make a batch of Crystallized Ginger and keep it in the freezer to have on hand to garnish all kinds of desserts like this custard.

A B C D

The best part of pumpkin pie is the filling—and it's gluten-free. Just bake the sweet creamy mixture in ramekins and then top them with whipped cream and a little crystallized ginger.

Strawberry Pie Ⓥ ⒧

Special Health Benefits

Not only are strawberries beautiful and delicious, they're also very good for you. Ounce for ounce, strawberries have more vitamin C than citrus fruit. According to the American Cancer Society, foods rich in vitamin C may lower the risk of cancers of the gastrointestinal tract. And one cup of strawberries has only 50 calories.

Ingredients

1 cup gluten-free all-purpose flour such as Domata Living™ Flour

½ cup sugar

1 teaspoon baking powder

⅓ cup butter, melted and cooled

1 beaten egg

2 tablespoons carbonated water

1 cup sugar

2 tablespoons cornstarch

1½ cups water

2 tablespoons light-color corn syrup

3 tablespoons dry strawberry gelatin such as Jell-O®

6 cups strawberries, hulled and sliced

Directions

1 Preheat oven to 325°F. For crust, in a large bowl mix flour, ½ cup sugar, and baking powder.

2 In a custard cup or small bowl mix melted butter, egg, and carbonated water. Add to flour mixture and stir until combined. Dough will be soft. See Photo A.

3 Pat dough onto bottom and side of a 9-inch pie plate. See Photo B. Bake for 15 minutes. Cool.

4 For glaze, in a small saucepan stir together 1 cup sugar and cornstarch. Add water and corn syrup. Bring to boiling, stirring constantly. Boil for 1 minute. Remove from heat and add gelatin, stirring until dissolved. Cool until room temperature.

5 Layer one-third of the strawberries into cooled crust. Pour one-third of the glaze over strawberries. See Photo C. Continue adding strawberries and glaze until all berries and glaze are used. See Photo D. Chill for at least 2 hours before serving. *Serves 9.*

Nutrition Per Serving:
322 calories, 8g fat, 4g saturated fat, 30mg cholesterol, 81mg sodium, 64g carbohydrate, 3g fiber, 2g protein

A

B

C

D

When berry season rolls around, use those precious berries to make this pie. It's a work of art—colorful, luscious, and gluten-free.

Blackberry-Filled Cake Roll Ⓥ

Make Ahead and Freeze for Later
To get a jump start on your next party dessert, make the cake and leave it rolled in the towel. Seal it in a large freezer bag and keep it frozen for up to 4 weeks. When it's party time, thaw the cake, add the filling, and serve.

Nutrition Per Serving:
426 calories, 14g fat, 8g saturated fat, 146mg cholesterol, 230mg sodium, 72g carbohydrate, 2g fiber, 6g protein

Ingredients

6 eggs
2 cups granulated sugar
⅔ cup water
2 teaspoons vanilla
2 cups gluten-free all-purpose flour such as Domata Living™ Flour
2 teaspoons baking powder
½ teaspoon salt
Powdered sugar
1 recipe Blackberry Filling
Chopped pistachios, fresh mint sprigs, and/or blackberries (optional)

Directions

1 Preheat oven to 375°F. Line a 15x10-inch jelly-roll pan with parchment paper. Grease and set aside. In a large bowl beat eggs with an electric mixer on high speed about 5 minutes or until very thick and lemon colored. See Photo A.

2 Gradually beat in granulated sugar. Beat in water and vanilla on low speed. Gradually add flour, baking powder, and salt, beating just until batter is smooth. Pour batter onto parchment paper in pan and spread to corners. See Photo B.

3 Bake for 12 to 15 minutes or until a wooden toothpick comes out clean inserted in the center. Using knife, loosen cake from edges of pan; invert onto a clean thin towel sprinkled with powdered sugar. See Photo C. Carefully remove paper; trim any stiff or crusty edges.

4 While hot, roll cake and towel together from long side. See Photo D. Cool on a wire rack.

5 Unroll cake and remove towel. Spread cake with Blackberry Filling. See Photo E. Reroll cake and dust with more powdered sugar. Wrap in foil or waxed paper. Chill for at least 2 hours before cutting. If desired garnish with pistachios, mint, and/or blackberries. *Serves 12.*

Blackberry Filling

1 Place 2 cups blackberries in a blender. Cover and blend until puréed. Press through a sieve; discard seeds. In a large bowl beat 1½ cups whipping cream with electric mixer until thick. Fold in ½ cup powdered sugar and puréed blackberries.

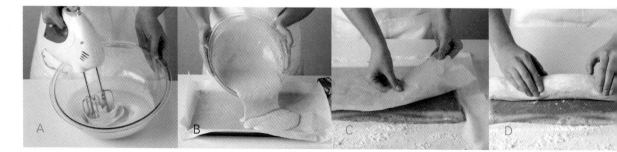

A   B   C   D

This extraordinary dessert showcases a tender, gluten-free cake wrapped around an irresistible blackberry and whipped cream filling. If you like, you also can make it with strawberries or raspberries.

E

When people begin a gluten-free diet,

they often give up desserts because most desserts contain gluten. Making pies or other desserts that require flour are now a little easier to make. Luckily, with all the new gluten-free flours and products available today, delicious gluten-free desserts are a reality. But choosing desserts that are naturally gluten-free is even an easier, faster way to find that sweet finish at the end of the meal. Here's a list of gluten-free desserts that require very few changes:

- Ice Cream: Many ice creams are gluten-free, especially vanilla-flavored ice creams. "All natural" does not necessarily indicate that a product in gluten-free, so be sure to read the label carefully.

- Cheesecake: Cheesecake recipes usually contain a few tablespoons of flour, but it can easily be replaced with cornstarch. Because cornstarch is a more powerful thickener than wheat flour, however, use only half the amount of cornstarch.

- Puddings: Puddings are starch-thickened products, so cornstarch can be used as the thickener. In fact, many boxed puddings, including instant puddings, are already gluten-free.

- Gelatins: Gelatin is a protein, not a starch as many people believe. Therefore gelatin desserts are gluten-free unless a gluten ingredient is added to them.

- Fruits: Decades ago, fruits were very expensive and treasured parts of the meal, so they often were served as a fancy sweet treat for dessert. Try ending your meal with a beautiful orange or delicious peach.

- Crisps: Traditional crisps are topped with flour or oatmeal, but they serve no function except for crunchiness and texture. Gluten-free flours are an easy solution to making crisps gluten-free.

- Custard: Made from eggs and milk, there is no need for gluten in custards. Custards provide a light, nutritious end to a meal.

Elizabeth says:

Pastries and pie crusts are especially difficult to make gluten-free. Be sure to keep everything cold while mixing, and store in the refrigerator for an hour before attempting to roll out the pastry. If you can't successfully roll out the pie crust, use your fingers to push the crust into the pan.

9 Family Favorites

Add a Flavor Variation

For a lively flavor boost, add ½ teaspoon dried sage or basil to the flour mixture. Then coat the chicken pieces as directed. Make an easy sweet-and-sour dipping sauce to serve with the chicken by mixing equal parts honey and gluten-free mustard.

Chicken Nuggets **HP**

Ingredients

2 skinless, boneless chicken breasts
1 cup brown rice flour
1 cup potato flour
3 tablespoons tapioca flour
1 teaspoon salt
2 eggs
½ cup whole milk
¼ cup canola oil

Directions

1 Wash chicken and remove any remaining skin or bone. Cut chicken into 1-inch pieces and set aside.

2 In a 1-gallon zipper-style plastic bag mix the rice flour, potato flour, and tapioca flour. Set aside.

3 In a small bowl beat eggs. Stir in milk and set aside. In a medium skillet heat oil over medium heat.

4 Dip chicken, a few pieces at a time, in the egg mixture. See Photo A. Take the chicken out of the egg mixture; place inside the bag with the flour mixture. See Photo B. Seal bag and shake it well so flour mixture thoroughly coats the chicken. Repeat to coat all of the chicken with the egg mixture and the flour mixture.

5 Fry the chicken, a few pieces at time, in the hot oil about 6 minutes or until golden brown and thoroughly cooked, turning once. See Photo C. *Serves 6.*

Nutrition Per Serving:
423 calories, 11g fat, 3g saturated fat, 127mg cholesterol, 301mg sodium, 53g carbohydrate, 3g fiber, 27g protein

Elizabeth says:
The combination of flours in this recipe makes for batter-coated chicken pieces that fry up crunchy yet tender and delicious.

Crisp, moist, and full of flavor, these little morsels of chicken will bring your family to the table without even calling them.

Fruit Pizza Ⓥ

Special Health Benefits

The beautiful colors of the fruits on this pizza signal that it's a wholesome thing to eat. In general, the brighter the colors of the fruits, the more nutrients they contain.

Freeze for Later

Bake a couple of these crusts to tuck in the freezer for later. Simply bake and cool the crusts. Then wrap each one in foil and freeze it for up to 3 weeks.

Nutrition Per Serving:
440 calories, 23g fat, 14g saturated fat, 79mg cholesterol, 376mg sodium, 57g carbohydrate, 2g fiber, 5g protein

Ingredients

1¼ cups sugar

1 cup butter, softened

1 egg, beaten

3 cups gluten-free all-purpose flour such as Domata Living™ Flour

1 teaspoon baking soda

1 teaspoon salt

¼ cup carbonated water

1 teaspoon vanilla

1 8-ounce tub cream cheese

6 cups fruit pieces such as peeled mango, blueberries, strawberries, raspberries, peeled kiwifruit, and/or seedless grapes

Directions

1 Preheat oven to 350°F. Grease large baking sheets and set aside. In a large bowl stir together sugar and butter until well mixed. Add egg and mix well.

2 In a medium bowl combine flour, baking soda, and salt and mix well.

3 Add flour mixture to butter mixture, stirring until combined. Add carbonated water and vanilla and mix just until blended. Divide dough into 3 portions.

4 Place dough portions on greased baking sheets. Using your fingers, press and shape each dough portion into a circle about 9 inches in diameter. Build up edge of each dough circle. See Photo A.

5 Using a fork, make holes in the bottom of each dough circle. See Photo B. Bake about 15 minutes or until edges of crusts begin to brown. Cool on baking sheets on wire racks.

6 Spread cream cheese on top of the cooled crusts. See Photo C.

7 Arrange cut fruit on each crust as desired. See Photo D. Refrigerate until ready to serve. Makes 3 small pizzas. *Serves 12.*

Carol says:
This crust is sweet, yet crisp, and is a lovely complement to the beautiful fresh fruit of the season.

This eye-catching fruit pizza is bound to be the center of attention at any gathering. Mix and match different fruits each time you serve it.

Add a Flavor Variation

For a special treat, add ½ cup fresh blueberries or ¼ cup dried blueberries to the batter before you cook the pancakes.

Buckwheat Pancakes Ⓥ ⒧⒡ ⒲⒢

Ingredients

¾ cup buckwheat flour

¾ cup gluten-free all-purpose flour such as Domata Living™ Flour

2 tablespoons sugar

1 tablespoon baking powder

½ teaspoon salt

1½ cups milk

2 egg whites

¼ cup butter, melted

Directions

1 In a large bowl combine buckwheat flour, all-purpose flour, sugar, baking powder, and salt. Slowly pour milk, egg whites, and melted butter into flour mixture. Stir together until smooth.

2 Lightly oil a griddle or skillet and place over medium heat. For each pancake, pour ¼ cup of the batter onto hot griddle. Cook until done in center and brown, turning to brown on both sides. *Serves 6.*

Marcia says:

I make these pancakes on Saturday mornings. The kids love to put peanut butter and bananas between the cakes.

Serve these tender pancakes with crisp bacon or fresh fruit for a tasty breakfast or a light supper.

9

Nutrition Per Serving:

233 calories, 8g fat, 5g saturated fat, 22mg cholesterol, 486mg sodium, 35g carbohydrate, 2g fiber, 7g protein

Breakfast Sausages CF EF

Ingredients

12 gluten-free pork
   sausage links such
   as Johnsonville®
   Breakfast Links

½ cup chopped fresh
   peaches or ½ cup
   canned light peaches,
   drained and chopped

2 tablespoons pure
   maple syrup

Directions

1 In a small skillet cook sausages according to
package directions. Remove from skillet and drain
well. Discard fat from skillet.

2 Return sausages to skillet and add peaches
and syrup. Cook until heated through. Serve
immediately. *Serves 6.*

Carol says:
The mix of maple syrup and
peaches makes a wonderful
sweet glaze for the sausages.

**Add a Flavor
Variation**
*If peaches are out
of season or you
prefer another
fruit, try chopped
mangoes or
apples
instead.
Use
¼ cup
chopped
mango or ½ cup
chopped apple.*

These easy,
delicious sausages
go great with
scrambled eggs,
waffles, or
pancakes.

**Nutrition
Per Serving:**
121 calories, 9g fat,
3g saturated fat,
20mg cholesterol,
265mg sodium, 6g
carbohydrate, 0g
fiber, 4g protein

Pigs in a Blanket ⓗⓟ

Read the Label
Because they are a processed meat, many brands of hot dogs and frankfurters are not gluten-free. Oftentimes the package will be plainly marked "gluten-free." If not, be sure and check with the company before using.

Ingredients

1¼ cups gluten-free all-purpose flour such as Domata Living™ Flour

¼ cup yellow cornmeal

1 tablespoon baking powder

1 teaspoon sugar

½ teaspoon salt

¾ cup water

⅓ cup milk

1 egg, beaten

1¼ teaspoons olive oil

8 gluten-free fully cooked frankfurters such as John Morrell®

8 3x¼-inch strips Colby and Monterey Jack cheese

Directions

1 Preheat oven to 400°F. In a medium bowl combine flour, cornmeal, baking powder, sugar, and salt. In a small bowl combine the water, milk, egg, and oil.

2 Make a well in the center of the dry ingredients and pour in egg mixture. Mix well.

3 Divide dough into 8 portions. Lightly grease a baking sheet and lay a frankfurter on baking sheet. Flour hands and pat out 1 dough portion into a rectangle about 1 inch longer than the frankfurter. See Photo A.

4 Make a slit down the middle of the frankfurter and put cheese strip into the slit. See Photo B.

5 Turn the dough to wrap crosswise around the frankfurter and secure with a wooden toothpick. See Photo C. Repeat with the remaining dough portions, frankfurters, and cheese strips.

6 Place all 8 wrapped frankfurters back on the baking sheet. Bake about 12 minutes or until the dough turns golden brown and the cheese melts. Remove toothpick before serving. *Serves 8.*

Nutrition Per Serving:
301 calories, 17g fat, 7g saturated fat, 57mg cholesterol, 899mg sodium, 27g carbohydrate, 1g fiber, 10g protein

Elizabeth says:

You might notice that gluten-free flours don't brown as much as wheat flour. Why? They contain fewer proteins and sugars, both of which are needed for browning.

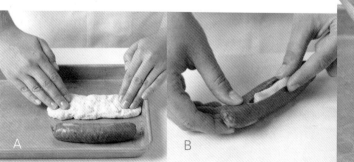

A   B   C

Serve this kid-favorite meal with gluten-free chips or apple chips. Add a glass of milk and the meal is complete.

Cake Donuts Ⓥ

Read the Label

When using any small candies such as sprinkles for garnish, be sure to check the label. While many bakery candies are gluten-free, they may have been manufactured in a plant that also handles products with gluten. The label may indicate this. Avoid any products processed in this way. If you're unsure, check with the company.

Nutrition Per Serving:
286 calories, 14g fat, 3g saturated fat, 27mg cholesterol, 234mg sodium, 37g carbohydrate, 1g fiber, 3g protein

Ingredients

½ cup milk

⅓ cup sugar

1 egg

2 tablespoons butter, melted

2¼ cups gluten-free all-purpose flour such as King Arthur Flour™

2 teaspoons baking powder

½ teaspoon salt

⅛ teaspoon ground nutmeg

Vegetable oil for frying

1 recipe Chocolate Glaze (optional)

1 recipe Vanilla Glaze (optional)

Gluten-free multi-colored sprinkles (optional)

Directions

1 In a medium bowl stir together the milk, sugar, egg, and butter. In another medium bowl combine flour, baking powder, salt, and nutmeg. Gradually add the milk mixture to the flour mixture, stirring until smooth (do not overmix). See Photo A.

2 On a lightly floured surface roll out dough until ½ inch thick. See Photo B. Use a floured donut cutter to cut out donuts.

3 Pour vegetable oil into an electric skillet, deep fryer, or cast-iron skillet to a depth of about 2 inches. Heat oil to 350°F. Slide donuts into hot oil. See Photo C. Cook about 4 minutes or until golden brown on both sides, turning each donut as it browns and rises to the surface. See Photo D. Carefully remove donuts from oil and place on a wire rack to cool. If desired, dip donuts into Chocolate Glaze or Vanilla Glaze and top with colored sprinkles. Makes about 20 donuts. *Serves 10.*

Vanilla Glaze: In a small bowl combine 2 cups powdered sugar and 3 tablespoons milk. Mix until creamy. Makes about 1 cup glaze.

Chocolate Glaze: In a small saucepan mix 6 tablespoons milk, 6 tablespoons sugar, and 3 tablespoons butter. Bring to boiling. Remove from heat and stir in ½ cup gluten-free semisweet chocolate chips. Cool slightly before using. Makes about 1 cup glaze.

9

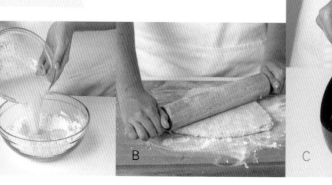

A   B   C

No matter how you serve them—plain or glazed, with or without sprinkles, these tender, golden donuts will please everyone in the family.

Blueberry Buckle V

Add a Flavor Variation

This coffee cake-style treat can be made with other fruits such as peaches. Substitute 2 cups sliced fresh peaches or canned drained peaches for the blueberries. If you're using fresh peaches, add 1 teaspoon lemon juice to the fruit before mixing.

When guests come for the weekend, serve them your favorite coffee or tea and squares of this luscious, fruity buckle for a midday snack.

9

Nutrition Per Serving:
340 calories, 14g fat, 5g saturated fat, 46mg cholesterol, 180mg sodium, 52g carbohydrate, 2g fiber, 4g protein

Ingredients

2 cups gluten-free all-purpose flour such as Domata Living™ Flour

2½ teaspoons baking powder

½ cup butter

¾ cup sugar

2 eggs

½ cup buttermilk

2 tablespoons carbonated water

2 cups fresh or frozen blueberries

½ cup gluten-free all-purpose flour such as Domata Living™ Flour

½ cup sugar

½ teaspoon ground cinnamon

¼ cup butter

Directions

1 Preheat oven to 350°F. Grease bottom and ½ inch up sides of a 9x9- or 8x8-inch baking pan; set aside. In a medium bowl combine the 2 cups flour and baking powder. Set aside.

2 In a medium bowl beat the ½ cup butter with an electric mixer on medium speed for 30 seconds. Add the ¾ cup sugar. Beat on medium to high speed until light and fluffy. Add eggs; beat well. In another bowl mix buttermilk with carbonated water. Alternately add flour mixture and buttermilk mixture to beaten egg mixture, beating just until combined.

3 Spoon batter into prepared pan. Sprinkle with blueberries. For topping, in a small bowl combine the ½ cup flour, the ½ cup sugar, and the cinnamon. Using a pastry blender, cut in the ¼ cup butter until mixture resembles coarse crumbs; sprinkle over blueberries. Bake for 50 to 60 minutes or until topping is golden brown. Serve warm. *Serves 12.*

Popcorn Balls **V** **LF** **EF** **WG**

Ingredients

6 tablespoons butter

3 cups gluten-free marshmallows

3 tablespoons dry gluten-free gelatin such as such as Jell-O® (any flavor)

3 quarts popped popcorn

Butter

Directions

1 In a medium saucepan melt the 6 tablespoons butter. Stir in marshmallows and gelatin. Cook over low heat, stirring constantly, until marshmallows are melted.

2 Place popcorn in a very large bowl. Gradually add the marshmallow mixture, stirring constantly. Grease your hands with additional butter and shape mixture into popcorn balls. Place on waxed paper to cool. *Serves 12.*

Marcia says:
I make these Popcorn Balls in various colors and serve them at birthday parties—I just change the gelatin color to fit the party theme.

The Cost
Because popcorn is economical, this recipe is really a bargain. Even when you count the cost of the other ingredients, these sweets still come in at only about 20¢ a serving. They are cheaper than a candy bar!

Looking for a fun family activity? Gather everyone together to make these oh-so-sweet popcorn treats.

Nutrition Per Serving:
130 calories, 6g fat, 4g saturated fat, 15mg cholesterol, 22mg sodium, 19g carbohydrate, 1g fiber, 2g protein

Deciding to live gluten-free will require commitment from your whole family. Although other family members may not need to restrict gluten from their diets, they will need to follow a few rules to support your lifestyle. The following suggestions are simple and will go a long way toward enabling you to eat gluten-free while allowing other family members to eat their favorite foods.

- Organize your pantry to separate gluten-free food items from any containing gluten. Use different drawers, different cupboards, even different rooms if your kitchen space allows. Store the gluten-free foods above the foods containing gluten to avoid an accidental spill which would require the replacement of your entire gluten-free stockpile.

> **Marcia says:**
> Let family members know you appreciate that they are supportive of your gluten-free diet and that you realize it will mean changes in everyone's lives.

- Designate a safe counter top to place your gluten-free foods or restrict the foods containing gluten to a counter top that you will avoid. This greatly reduces potential contamination by unseen crumbs and flour dust.

- Double up on equipment that commonly comes in contact with bread or other baked goods, and clearly label one "Gluten-Free." Toasters, waffle irons, sandwich makers, and cutting boards are all indispensable for a varied gluten-free diet—but only if they have never been in contact with gluten. It only takes one piece of wheat bread in your gluten-free toaster to render it useless. Clearly label and keep this equipment within a designated area, if possible.

- Train your family to use serving utensils carefully. Foods that require a utensil to remove a serving out of a larger container, such as peanut butter or jelly, require special attention because a contaminated utensil can ruin the entire product. You could double up on these foods to be safe, but the sheer number of these items in most kitchens will likely make duplication cost-prohibitive. The solution is to designate a serving utensil each meal that will be the only one used for dishing out a specific product.

- Be sure everyone always washes hands and wipes surfaces before getting out any food. Not only is this good hygiene, but it is a final line of defense against stray crumbs and flour particles.

Good to know: cooking basics

Starting a gluten-free diet means that you may be cooking more than you did before. Eating out is difficult and buying purchased gluten-free packaged foods is expensive. You will probably be eating more grains, beans, vegetables, and fruits. Knowing more about these ingredients and how to prepare them will help you become more confident when you are making the recipes. So enjoy cooking gluten-free—you'll feel better than you have ever felt before!

Grains

While everyone eats grains on a regular basis, individuals on a gluten-free diet must avoid four of the most common grains (wheat, barley, rye, and oats). However, this is an opportunity to try other delicious varieties of grains, including sorghum, amaranth, buckwheat, and quinoa. Grains contain starch, fiber, vitamins, minerals, are low in fat, and have a variety of flavors. Always choose whole grains when possible for a more nutritious meal.

The grains we have pictured here are only a few of the many grains that are easily found at supermarkets and health food stores.

Rice is a cheap, nutritious, versatile ingredient to always have on hand. White rice and brown rice are staples in a gluten-free diet. Instant white and brown rices are also gluten-free, and they cook much faster than their traditional counterparts. Some people may consider rice to be a boring ingredient, but look around the grocery store and try new types of rice. Short-grain and medium-grain rices, such as Arborio rice, are used in risotto and sticky rice recipes. Long-grain rice, such as Basmati, is used in most traditional recipes.

Wild rice is really a marsh grass—not a rice at all. But like true rice, it is gluten-free. It is high in protein, the amino acid lysine (which is unusual for a grain), and dietary fiber. It is also a good source of potassium, phosphorus, and vitamins thiamin, riboflavin, and niacin. Wild rice adds a delicious nutty flavor and crunchy texture to recipes.

Buckwheat, even though the name may suggest it, is not a wheat grain at all. It is actually a fruit seed related to rhubarb and sorrel. The protein in buckwheat contains eight essential amino acids and is high in lysine.

Native to South America, **quinoa** is found in tan and red varieties. It contains all the essential amino acids, making it an unusually complete protein source among plant foods. It is also a good source of dietary fiber, and contains significant phosphorus, iron, and magnesium.

Because it can be used in so many different ways, **amaranth** is often referred to as the "crop of the future". It is often served in South America with honey, molasses, or chocolate as a sweet treat.

Millet, a staple grain in Africa, is usually sold as birdseed in the U.S. However, it is fairly nutritious, very inexpensive, and easy to prepare. Millet has a bitter flavor, so it is usually mixed with other ingredients or flours.

Corn is a grain with which everyone is familiar. Corn is inexpensive, versatile, and represents a whole grain food. It can be served boiled on the cob, scalloped, buttered, or in meal form for muffins and breads and various other simple recipes.

Teff is a tiny grain that comes from an annual grass (a species of lovegrass) native to the northern Ethiopian Highlands of northeast Africa. It is high in dietary fiber as well as providing iron, protein, and calcium.

In many parts of the world **sorghum** has traditionally been used in unleavened bread, cookies, cakes, couscous, and malted beverages. The whole grain can be easily ground into sorghum flour. Some sorghum varieties are rich in antioxidants, and all sorghum varieties are gluten-free. Because of its neutral taste, sorghum absorbs other flavors very well.

Key to the Grains

1 Instant White Rice	**5** Wild Rice
2 Instant Brown Rice	**6** Amaranth
3 Teff	**7** Arborio Rice
4 Red Quinoa	**8** Millet

Legumes

The Leguminosae family contains over 20,000 species, including beans, peas, peanuts, soybeans, and lentils. In the U.S. people commonly consume only a few varieties, but eating a gluten-free diet is a great excuse for trying new delicious varieties. Legumes are a good source of protein, an excellent source of fiber, contain vitamins and minerals, and are very cheap and easy to store. Most legumes are very low in fat, with the exception of soybeans and peanuts.

Key to the Legumes

1 Garbanzo Beans
2 French Lentils
3 Split Peas
4 Red Lentils
5 Black-eyed Peas
6 Azuki Beans
7 Mung Beans

Garbanzo beans, also known as chickpeas, are an ancient bean from the Mediterranean. Now eaten across the world, they are delicious in soups, salads, or ground into hummus.

Originating in India, **lentils** are one of the oldest domesticated crops known. Lentils are very high in protein and contain one of the largest amounts of iron of any plant food. They are therefore especially important in vegetarian diets.

Black-eyed peas are a sign of good luck in many cultures. They have a long-standing tradition as a popular legume in the southern United States; they were very popular even during the American Revolution. Today known as "soul food", they are high in protein, calcium, vitamin A, and folic acid.

Azuki beans are popular in Japan and China, but they are fairly new to the United States. They are often served sweetened, as in baked products or ice cream.

Mung beans are commonly used in Asian cuisine. They are a very versatile ingredient and can be served in many ways. Mung beans sprouts are also popular.

Soybeans are available in several varieties, with some grown for human consumption and some grown for animal feed. Unlike most legumes, soybeans contain about 20% fat and no starch. Edamame, an immature soybean variety, is a legume that is gaining popularity. Tofu and soymilk are two other important soy products.

Split peas come in two varieties: green and yellow. The most common way Americans eat split peas is in split pea soup. Split peas contain B vitamins and are a great source of dietary fiber.

It is important to note that many legumes contain toxins, so when starting with dry legumes (as opposed to canned), it is important to always fully soak and fully cook legumes before eating. The toxins are released into the water when soaking and destroyed when cooked with heat.

Gluten-free Flours

One reason gluten-free baked products are so difficult to make is that wheat flour is an amazing food—it can create food products with many different characteristics. Baked products with wheat can be flaky, tender, chewy, crusty, airy and light, or dense and heavy. No other flour has all these characteristics, but many other flours have a few of these characteristics. Therefore, it makes sense to choose specific gluten-free flours that have the specific properties of the baked product you want to make. For a delicate cake, choose a flour mix with a high proportion of tapioca or potato flour. For a dense yeast bread, choose a dense, heavy flour mix with a high proportion of brown rice or bean flour.

How gluten-free flour is measured is very important because many of the types of flours that make up the all-purpose mix are light and can pack easily.

Depending on the make up of the flour, how you measure it may make a difference of ½ cup or more. In most cases it is best to spoon the flour into the measuring cup rather than using the measuring cup to scoop it from a canister or bag.

Read the Label

Anyone on a gluten-free diet knows the importance of reading nutrition labels and ingredient lists. Some words obviously indicate that gluten is in a product such as "wheat flour" or "wheat starch," but other words can be more difficult to decipher.

Although this ingredient list contains "food starch-modified," this product should be gluten-free because it specifies that it only contains soy, not wheat, in the Allergen List in bold. Calling the company would be the best way to double-check that the food is indeed gluten-free.

Nutrition Facts
Serving Size as packaged
1 1/3 Tbsp. (14g) as packaged
Servings Per Container about 8

Amount Per Serving	Dry Mix
Calories	50

	% Daily Value*
Total Fat 0g	0%
Sodium 80mg	3%
Total Carbohydrate 12g	4%
Sugars 7g	
Protein 0g	

*Percent Daily Values are based on a 2,000 calorie diet.

INGREDIENTS: SUGAR, CORNSTARCH, FOOD STARCH-MODIFIED, CITRIC ACID, SALT, NATURAL LEMON FLAVOR, YELLOW 5 LAKE, YELLOW 6 LAKE.
CONTAINS SOY.

Distributed by
ACH Food Companies, Inc.,
Memphis, TN 38016 USA
"SPICE ADVICE" 1-800-247-5251
www.durkee.com

Cholesterol	Less than	300mg	300mg
Sodium	Less than	2,400mg	2,400mg
Potassium		3,500mg	3,500mg
Total Carbohydrate		300g	375g
Dietary Fiber		25g	30g
Calories per gram: Fat 9 • Carbohydrate 4 • Protein 4			

INGREDIENTS: WHOLE GRAIN OATS, SUGAR, CORN SYRUP, OAT BRAN, RICE, HONEY, SOLUBLE WHEAT FIBER, MODIFIED CORN STARCH, SOY GRITS, MOLASSES, CORN FLOUR, NATURAL FLAVOR, SALT, ACACIA GUM, SOY PROTEIN ISOLATE, OAT FIBER, EVAPORATED CANE JUICE, MALT FLAVORING, HIGH FRUCTOSE CORN SYRUP, NIACINAMIDE, REDUCED IRON, BHT (PRESERVATIVE), PYRIDOXINE HYDROCHLORIDE (VITAMIN B6), THIAMIN HYDROCHLORIDE (VITAMIN B1), RIBOFLAVIN (VITAMIN B2), ASCORBIC ACID (VITAMIN C), VITAMIN A PALMITATE, FOLIC ACID, FERROUS FUMARATE, CALCIUM PANTOTHENATE, VITAMIN D, VITAMIN B12.

CONTAINS SOY AND WHEAT INGREDIENTS.

Distributed by Kellogg Sales Co.
Battle Creek, MI 49016 USA
®, TM, © 2009 Kellogg NA Co.

Exchange: 2 1/2 Carbohydrates, 1/2 Fat
The dietary exchanges are based on the *Choose Your Foods: Exchange Lists for Diabetes*, ©2008 by American Dietetic Association and American Diabetes Association.

The list of ingredients indicates gluten is in this product, and the Allergen List specifies that this product does contain wheat ingredients. This is definitely not gluten-free.

Dietary Fiber 0g		0%
Sugars 0g		
Protein 2g		

Vitamin A 0%	•	Vitamin C 0%
Calcium 0%	•	Iron 2%

*Percent Daily Values are based on a 2,000 calorie diet. Your daily values may be higher or lower depending on your calorie needs:

		Calories:	2,000	2,500
Total Fat	Less than		65g	80g
Saturated Fat			20g	25g
Cholesterol	Less than		300mg	300mg
Sodium	Less than		2,400mg	2,400mg
Total Carbohydrate			300g	375g
Dietary Fiber			25g	30g

INGREDIENTS: SPECIALTY FLOUR BLEND (RICE FLOUR, TAPIOCA STARCH), POTATO STARCH, WHOLE GRAIN BROWN RICE FLOUR.

This list of ingredients specifies exactly what flours are in this flour mix, but we cannot assume it is gluten-free unless it also says "gluten-free" somewhere on the package. Often many flours are milled in the same facility, and cross-contamination with gluten-containing flours is a definite possibility.

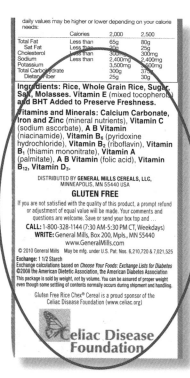

daily values may be higher or lower depending on your calorie needs:

		Calories	2,000	2,500
Total Fat	Less than		65g	80g
Sat Fat	Less than		20g	25g
Cholesterol	Less than		300mg	300mg
Sodium	Less than		2,400mg	2,400mg
Potassium			3,500mg	3,500mg
Total Carbohydrate			300g	375g
Dietary Fiber			25g	30g

Ingredients: Rice, Whole Grain Rice, Sugar, Salt, Molasses. Vitamin E (mixed tocopherols) and BHT Added to Preserve Freshness.

Vitamins and Minerals: Calcium Carbonate, Iron and Zinc (mineral nutrients), Vitamin C (sodium ascorbate), **A B Vitamin** (niacinamide), **Vitamin B6** (pyridoxine hydrochloride), **Vitamin B2** (riboflavin), **Vitamin B1** (thiamin mononitrate), **Vitamin A** (palmitate), **A B Vitamin** (folic acid), **Vitamin B12**, **Vitamin D3**.

DISTRIBUTED BY **GENERAL MILLS CEREALS, LLC,** MINNEAPOLIS, MN 55440 USA

GLUTEN FREE

If you are not satisfied with the quality of this product, a prompt refund or adjustment of equal value will be made. Your comments and questions are welcome. Save or send your box top and ...

CALL: 1-800-328-1144 (7:30 AM-5:30 PM CT, Weekdays)
WRITE: General Mills, Box 200, Mpls, MN 55440
www.GeneralMills.com

© 2010 General Mills   May be mfg. under U.S. Pat. Nos. 6,210,720 & 7,021,525

Exchange: 1 1/2 Starch
Exchange calculations based on *Choose Your Foods: Exchange Lists for Diabetes* ©2008 the American Dietetic Association, the American Diabetes Association
This package is sold by weight, not by volume. You can be assured of proper weight even though some settling of contents normally occurs during shipment and handling.

Gluten Free Rice Chex® Cereal is a proud sponsor of the Celiac Disease Foundation (www.celiac.org)

Celiac Disease Foundation

The words "Gluten Free" on this label make it easy to know that this ingredient is safe to eat for celiacs.

Emergency Substitutions—Always Use Gluten-Free Products

If you don't have:	Substitute:
Baking powder, 1 teaspoon	½ teaspoon cream of tartar plus ¼ teaspoon baking soda
Balsamic vinegar, 1 tablespoon	1 tablespoon gluten-free cider vinegar or red wine vinegar plus ½ teaspoon sugar
Broth, beef or chicken, 1 cup	1 cube gluten-free instant beef or chicken bouillon or 1 teaspoon gluten-free paste-style bouillon plus 1 cup hot water
Butter, 1 cup	1 cup shortening plus ¼ teaspoon salt, if desired
Buttermilk, 1 cup	1 tablespoon lemon juice or vinegar plus enough milk to make 1 cup (let stand 5 minutes before using) or 1 cup plain yogurt
Chocolate, semisweet, 1 ounce	3 tablespoons gluten-free semisweet chocolate pieces, or 1 ounce unsweetened chocolate plus 1 tablespoon granulated sugar, or 1 tablespoon unsweetened cocoa powder plus 1 teaspoon sugar and 2 teaspoons shortening
Chocolate, unsweetened, 1 ounce	3 tablespoons unsweetened cocoa powder plus 1 tablespoon cooking oil or shortening, melted
Corn syrup (light-color), 1 cup	1 cup granulated sugar plus ¼ cup water
Garlic, 1 clove	½ teaspoon bottled minced garlic or ⅛ teaspoon garlic powder
Ginger, grated fresh, 1 teaspoon	¼ teaspoon ground ginger
Half-and-half or light cream, 1 cup	1 tablespoon melted butter or margarine plus enough whole milk to make 1 cup
Onion, chopped, ½ cup	2 tablespoons dried minced onion or ½ teaspoon onion powder
Sour cream, dairy, 1 cup	1 cup gluten-free plain yogurt
Sugar, granulated, 1 cup	1 cup packed brown sugar or 1 cup sifted powdered sugar
Sugar, brown, 1 cup packed	1 cup granulated sugar plus 1 tablespoon molasses
Tomato juice, 1 cup	½ cup tomato sauce plus ½ cup water
Tomato sauce, 2 cups	¾ cup tomato paste plus 1 cup water
Yeast, active dry, 1 package	About 2¼ teaspoons active dry yeast

Preparing Fruits and Vegetables

Eating gluten-free may mean that you are eating more fruits and vegetables. Here are some tips on how to cut and use many common fruits and vegetables that you might use in your kitchen. You don't need a lot of fancy gadgets to prepare fruits and vegetables for eating or using in your favorite recipes.

Coring an Apple

There are many types of apple corers on the market. Most are sharp at one end designed to penetrate the core of the apple.

After the corer has gone into the apple, pull the corer out and the core will remain inside the corer.

Coring an Apple

To core an apple without an apple corer, first cut the apple in half. Then with the cut side down, slice again with hand on top of knife. Remove core area from each apple quarter.

Cutting a Mango

Mangoes have a large flat seed in the middle. The flat side of the seed runs parallel to the "cheeks" of the mango. Using a sharp knife cut off one cheek of the mango.

Use the knife to cut off the other cheek. These two cheeks are the areas where the majority of the edible fruit is located.

Use a sharp knife to make about 1-inch cuts across the flesh of the mango. Then cut across those lines the other way, forming small square shapes.

Pull the skin side of the mango back to force the square sections to pop forward. Then use a knife to cut the squares of fruit away from the skin.

Cutting Citrus

Slicing citrus fruits such as oranges, lemons, limes, or grapefruit is easy. Just remember to cut the fruit with the stem to the side. Make the slices as thin or thick as you like. Remove any seeds if necessary.

Zesting Citrus

Zesting fruits such as oranges or lemons requires a small grater or a zester—either tool will work well. Be sure the fruit is washed and dried. With a piece of waxed paper under the area, rub the fruit lightly over the grater. Catch the zest on the paper. Avoid grating into the white membrane.

Draining Large Fruits or Vegetables

If the pieces of the fruit or vegetables are large enough, simply use a spoon to hold back the fruit as you drain the juice into a saucer. Of course, a mesh strainer will work as well.

Draining Small Fruits or Vegetables

If the vegetables are small such as corn or peas, drain using a fork. Simply hold the fork at the edge of the can and drain the liquid into a saucer or other container. You can also use a mesh strainer.

Cutting Hot Peppers

If cutting hot peppers, always wear gloves to protect your hands, which could later touch eyes and cause intense burning. If you don't have gloves available, use a plastic sandwich bag on your hand. Cut the pepper in half, and remove as many seeds as possible.

Contrary to popular belief, the hottest part of the pepper is actually the inside flesh of the pepper, not the seeds or the core. The finer you chop the pepper, the more heat is released. For mild flavor, chop in large pieces, but for hot flavor, chop finely.

All About Eggs

Known as "Nature's Perfect Food," eggs really are incredible little packages of nutrition. Eggs contain a plethora of nutrients often lacking in gluten-free diets. Eggs contain B vitamins and vitamin D. Eggs are a great source of protein, and egg protein is rated the highest quality protein of any food. One large egg contains only 70 calories, 5 grams of fat, and many vitamins and minerals including vitamin D, vitamin B12, and choline. In fact, eggs contain almost every vitamin and mineral humans need except vitamin C.

Cracking and Separating an Egg

Firmly tap the egg on the counter, not on the side of the bowl, to avoid getting shells into the egg. One swift tap is all you need for a straight crack on the egg.

Carefully pull the two sides of the egg apart. If any pieces of shell land in the bowl, remove them with your finger or a spoon.

To separate an egg, gently pour the egg yolk back and forth between the two shell halves. The white will naturally separate from the yolk and drop into the bowl.

Hard-Cooking Eggs

Place eggs in a saucepan. Cover with cold water until the water is 1 inch above the tops of the eggs. Bring the eggs to a boil and let boil 1 minute. Cover pan and remove from heat.

Let the covered pan sit for 15 to 17 minutes. Then immediately pour the hot water out of pan and run cold water over eggs until eggs are cool to touch.

If not using eggs immediately, store eggs in the shell in the refrigerator for up to 1 week. If using eggs immediately, carefully peel eggs, starting with the larger end of the egg.

Recipe Egg Terms

Beat eggs slightly means to use a fork or whisk to beat the whole eggs until the yolk and white are combined and no streaks remain.

Beat egg yolks means to beat the egg yolks with an electric mixer on high speed for about five minutes or until they are thick and lemon-color. This method is often used for making sponge cakes or cake rolls.

Beat egg whites until the "soft peak" stage means that the beaten egg whites should form peaks with tips that curl over when the beaters are lifted out of the bowl.

Beat egg whites until the "stiff peak" stage means that the beaten egg whites should form peaks with tips that stand up straight when the beaters are lifted out of the bowl.

Making Meringue

A meringue is simply an egg white foam mixed with sugar. There are several tips important to making a successful, voluminous meringue. Do not use a plastic bowl because it may have fat or oil residue trapped in the plastic, and egg whites will not foam in the presence of fat. For the largest volume meringues use fresh, room temperature eggs, not eggs cold from refrigeration. Add a small amount of cream of tartar to improve the stability of the foam.

Begin by placing egg whites in a clean glass or metal bowl. Mix on high speed until the egg whites look foamy. Add half of the sugar and continue beating on high speed. The volume of the egg whites rapidly will begin to increase.

Add the remaining sugar and beat on high speed until the soft peak stage. Stop mixing the meringue here if using for pies or angel food cakes. Follow baking instructions for each specific recipe.

If desired, continue beating the meringue until the stiff peak stage. Use the meringue at this stage for macaroons, decorations, or topping cakes. Follow baking instructions for each specific recipe.

Making Sauces and Glazes

Sauces and glazes are delicious and there is no reason they need to contain gluten. However, most purchased sauces and glazes, such as cream soups, gravies, and purchased frostings do contain gluten. Making a simple white sauce or creating a powdered sugar glaze is really very simple. Knowing how to make your own sauces and glazes will save you time and money, as well as guarantee that they are indeed gluten-free.

Making a White Sauce

For 2 cups of white sauce, mix 2 tablespoons cornstarch with ½ cup of cold milk.

Stir well to separate the starch granules in the milk. Using cold milk, not hot milk, prevents lumps from forming in the white sauce.

Heat 1½ cups milk, 2 tablespoons butter, ½ teaspoon salt, and ¼ teaspoon pepper. Pour cornstarch/milk mixture slowly into the warm milk.

Heat on medium heat, stirring continuously until mixture is thickened and bubbly. Boil 1 minute, stirring constantly, then remove from heat.

Making a Powdered Sugar Glaze

In a small bowl mix together 2 cups powdered sugar, 3 tablespoons milk, and 1 tablespoon melted butter. Beat until smooth.

Place small plastic bag in measuring cup and open top. Pour glaze mixture into the bag.

Use scissors to cut off a tiny corner of the plastic bag to make a small piping spout.

Lay cookies, scones, or other items to be drizzled in a row on waxed paper and squeeze the glaze over the items, moving the bag quickly. Let dry.

Making Gluten-free Croutons

Croutons add extra flavor and texture to soups and salads and make them even more inviting. Even though croutons are usually made from wheat bread, they are very easy to make gluten-free. When making croutons, make extra for later. Simply keep them in your freezer to have on hand for special soups and salads.

Making Croutons

Cut slices of gluten-free bread into about 1-inch cubes.	In a skillet, heat 2 tablespoons butter. Add croutons to hot skillet.	Fry croutons on both sides until lightly browned, about 2 minutes on a side.

Basic Baking Tips

While baking gluten-free is a bit more challenging than preparing other gluten-free foods, many of the same baking principles apply to both gluten-free and wheat flour recipes. Making sure that a cake or bread is done can be tricky. Try this simple method, below left.

Greasing a pan is easy. Just use a little butter and a piece of waxed paper. See below, right.

Testing for Doneness

Greasing a Pan

To test to see if a cake is done cooking, insert a dry toothpick into the center of the cake. If there is wet batter on the toothpick, return the cake to the oven for a few more minutes.

If the toothpick comes out clean, the cake is done. Remove from oven and allow to cool on a rack.

Place a small piece of butter in a piece of waxed paper and rub the butter on the inside of the baking pan.

Herbs

Eating gluten-free means that you may be using more fresh herbs in some of your recipes. Some dried herb mixes do contain gluten. Fresh herbs are naturally gluten-free and add appetizing color and flavor to many recipes. There are dozens of fresh herbs to choose from. Here are a few that are commonly used.

Basil: This herb brings its much-loved flavor and aroma to sauces, salads, and, of course, pesto. There are many types of basil including lemon, cinnamon, and anise. They all possess the basic basil flavor, plus the flavor for which they are named.

Bay Leaves: Usually found in the form of whole, dried leaves, bay leaves are used in soups and stews. The aromatic and woodsy flavor is easily recognized. Bay leaves should be added to the dish whole—never crumbled—and always discarded before serving the dish.

Chives: This long slender green herb tastes like mild onion. After chives are cut they will grow back—just like grass. This mild and easy-to-grow herb tastes great chopped and sprinkled over salads, egg dishes, on potatoes, or in dressings.

Cilantro: This herb is also known as fresh coriander, leaf coriander, or Chinese parsley. Cilantro brings an aromatic flavor to many dishes. Often used in Asian specialties and Indian sauces, it is also used in Mexican salsas. Cilantro looks like parsley but with a flatter leaf.

Dill: The delicate taste of this familiar herb is suited to many dishes. It is excellent with eggs, fish, seafood, and vegetables. Dill can be used fresh or the seeds can be used in dressings or to flavor meats as well. Dried dill is often called "Dill Weed" when packaged.

Fennel: This herb has a licorice flavor and grows to look much like dill. The fennel bulb is also used in many dishes.

Lemon Balm: This fast-growing herb has a strong lemon scent and flavor and can be used in teas, sauces, and as a garnish.

Marjoram: Very similar to oregano, it has a sweeter, milder flavor. It can be used to season almost any meat and vegetable dish.

Mint: Mint has a sweet, refreshing flavor with a cool aftertaste. There are many kinds of mint. Peppermint has a sharp, pungent flavor, while spearmint is more delicate. Mint makes a great edible garnish for many desserts, and it is a nice addition to many drinks. An important ingredient in tabbouleh, try it in other salads and salad dressings as well.

Oregano: This popular and easily-found herb is often used in pizza and pasta. It has a robust, pungent flavor. Try it in soups and sauces as well.

Parsley: This favorite herb brings its mild, fresh taste to almost any dish. Used often as a garnish, try using it in stews, meats, soups, and salads. Flat-leaf parsley (also called Italian parsley) has a milder flavor than the curly-leaf variety. Generally either will work in recipes that call for parsley.

Key to the Herbs	
1 Dill	**6** Oregano
2 Basil	**7** Rosemary
3 Thyme	**8** Sage
4 Chives	**9** Mint
5 Curled Parsley	

Rosemary: This herb has almost a piney or perfume-like smell and taste. The leaves of this herb are almost needlelike—much like a pine needle. It is often used with potatoes, pork, lamb, and beef.

Sage: Used to season poultry, pork, and stuffing, this herb has sometimes been described as having a musty or bitter flavor. It also compliments vegetables.

Tarragon: Often used in French cuisine, tarragon has an aromatic, licorice-like flavor. It compliments poultry, most fish, grilled meats, and works well in salad dressings.

Thyme: Sometimes described as minty or lemony in flavor, thyme seasons chicken, vegetables, and sauces.

Using Fresh Herbs and Dried Herbs:
Using fresh herbs in your recipes is always best. They add flavor that can't be matched by dried herbs. If you don't have an herb garden of your own, try buying fresh herbs at a farmer's market or supermarket.

If a recipe calls for snipped fresh herbs, start with clean, dry herbs. With kitchen shears or scissors, simply cut the herbs, into small, uniform pieces using short, quick strokes. When the stalks are tough, as is the case with rosemary or some lemon balms, don't use the stalks. Snip herbs just before adding them to a recipe to get their maximum flavor.

If a recipe calls for dried herbs and you wish to substitute fresh, use three times the amount called for. For example, if the recipe calls for 1 tablespoon of a dried herb, use 3 tablespoons of the fresh herb. Exceptions include fresh rosemary which can become overpowering if too much is used.

Growing Your Own Herb Garden:
Growing your own herb garden is very easy and can make it fun to use fresh herbs. Start with a large low pot with adequate drainage. Fill it with fine potting soil. Sprinkle the seeds of the desired herbs on top of the soil. (Most herb seeds are very tiny.) Water gently. Mark each group of seeds with a tag or marker to identify the herb as it grows. Then carefully cover the seeds and water carefully again. Put the pot in a sunny location.

In no time you will have an herb garden with fresh herbs that you can enjoy any time of the year.

Slicing, Dicing, and More
- **Chop** means to cut foods with a sharp knife or food processor into fine, medium, or coarse irregular pieces.
- **Cube** means to cut food into small uniform cube-like pieces, usually ½ inch on all sides.
- **Dice** means to cut food into smaller uniform pieces, usually ⅛ to ¼ inch on all sides.
- **Julienne** means to cut food into thin strips (almost like match sticks) about 2 inches long. This is often done when cutting carrots or sweet peppers.
- **Mince** means to chop a food into very tiny irregular pieces.
- **Slice** means to cut food into flat, thin pieces such as slicing a cucumber or tomato.
- **Snip** means to use kitchen scissors to snip pieces of herb from the stem.

Lifestyle: living gluten-free

Eating gluten-free requires a change in your lifestyle. It means making changes in the way you cook, choosing different foods to eat, planning new menus, meeting your nutritional needs, and finding restaurants to frequent. Your gluten-free lifestyle takes cooperation from your family as well—and the changes you make will be good for all of you.

Guide to Eating Out Gluten-free

Eating out is a difficult task for individuals on a gluten-free diet. A list of menu ingredients is often not available, and the staff may not understand what "gluten-free" really means. Eating off of a "gluten-free menu" does not guarantee a gluten-free meal. Here are some tips to make eating out a pleasant and truly gluten-free experience:

- Take charge and ask questions. This may be difficult for shy individuals, but asking questions is the key to not getting sick. Ask your server if he/she understands what gluten is and how to avoid it, and don't be afraid to talk to the manager or chef if you think your server is unsure of how to handle your food.

- Memorize the foods and ingredients that are gluten-free, as well as those that are not gluten-free. If you know where gluten is likely "hiding," you can make smart choices when ordering off the menu.

- Consider a "Dining Card." These cards list all the common foods and ingredients that are gluten-free and not gluten-free, and they are available in dozens of languages. For more information about dining cards, see page 210. They can be a great help when eating out; simply hand the card to the server.

- Tell your server you are "very allergic to wheat." Although this statement isn't exactly true (celiac is not a true "allergy" and you cannot have barley, rye, or oats either), it simplifies what you need to share with your server but gets the point across. Then explain that you need to be very careful with what you eat. If your server still seems confused, ask for a manager.

- Protect yourself against cross-contamination. Make sure to remind your server that croutons cannot touch your salad, bread cannot touch your meal, and your food needs to be cooked in a clean pan. Otherwise the server may simply remove the croutons from a pre-made salad.

- Call ahead and speak to the manager or chef. Call the restaurant you are planning to go to and ask them if they have a gluten-free menu and are aware of how to cook a gluten-free meal. Chances are that they will either understand your questions right away (a good sign), or they will be confused and you will risk getting ill.

- Check on-line. Many restaurants, large and small, now have gluten-free menus on-line. Take the time to see if anything sounds appealing.

- If going to a new restaurant, have a snack before you eat out. In case there is nothing gluten-free on the menu, at least you won't starve while everyone else eats.

- Don't assume anything is gluten-free. Chefs often add "secret ingredients" that just may contain gluten. Question everything, no matter how basic.

- Once you've chosen what you want to order, ask detailed questions. Ask if the meat has been coated in flour, marinated, or if the grill used to cook your meat has also grilled bread or sandwiches. Ask if there are croutons on the salad. Ask if the potatoes are real or made from a box. Ask if the ice cream will come with cookies. Ask, ask, ask!

- If all else fails, wait to eat when you get home. You might be hungry for awhile while waiting at the restaurant, but it's better than becoming ill later.

Restaurants with Gluten-free Menus

There are hundreds of restaurants that offer gluten-free menus. Many are local restaurants, but there are some national chains as well. While this is not an endorsement for any restaurant, here is a list of some of the national restaurants that offer gluten-free menus at the time of this printing.

- Arby's®
- Baskin Robbins®
- Biaggi's
- BJ's Restaurant and Brewhouse
- Bonefish Grill®
- Boston Market®
- Boston's Gourmet Pizza®
- Burger King®
- Carabbas Italian Grill®
- Carl's Junior®
- Cheeseburger in Paradise
- Chili's®
- Chipotle Mexican Grill
- Cracker Barrel®
- Culver's®
- Dairy Queen®

- Don Pablo's®
- Fleming's® Prime Steakhouse and Wine Bar
- Garlic Jim's Famous Gourmet Pizza®
- Godfather's Pizza®
- Hardee's®
- HuHot Mongolian Grill®
- Legal Sea Foods™
- Lone Star Steakhouse®
- Maggiano's Little Italy®
- McDonald's®
- O'Charley's®
- The Old Spaghetti Factory
- On the Border®
- Outback Steakhouse®
- P.F. Chang's®

- Pizza Fusion™
- Red Robin®
- Ruby Tuesday
- Sam & Louie's™
- Shane's Rib Shack™
- Smoky Bone's Bar and Fire Grill
- Sonic® Drive-In
- Stonewood Grill and Tavern
- Subway®
- Taco Bell®
- Ted's Montana Grill®
- Uno Chicago Grill
- Wildfire®
- Wendy's®
- Z'Tejas Southwestern Grill

Menu Planning

Planning gluten-free menus is easy using the recipes in this book. Here are just a few ideas:

- Macaroni and Cheese
  Broiled Tomatoes
  Chocolate Cake

- Chicken Salad
  Cranberry-Applesauce Muffins
  Tapioca Pudding

- Fish Tacos
  Stir-Fried Kale
  Chocolate Chip Cookies

- Salmon Cakes
  Easy Cabbage Salad
  Lemon-Filled Cupcakes

- Tomato-Basil Soup
  Feta-Basil Bread
  Apple Crisp

- Lemon Chicken with Pea Pods
  Apple Walnut Salad
  Strawberry Pie

- Potato-Egg Bake
  Breakfast Sausages
  Cake Donuts

- Hoppin' John
  Glazed Pears
  Chewy Brownies

- Garbanzo Bean Soup
  Millet Flatbread
  Blackberry-Filled Cake Roll

- Veggie Pizza
  Greek Salad
  Chocolate Shake

- Split Pea Soup
  Buttery Corn Bread
  Rice Pudding

- Spaghetti and Meatballs
  Radish Salad
  Peanut Butter Cookies

- Asparagus Risotto
  Tomato Aspic
  Sugar Cookies

- Old-Fashioned Meat Loaf
  Sweet Potato Fries
  Waldorf Salad

- Quinoa Tabbouleh
  Tuscan Flatbread
  Pumpkin Custard

Food Safety

Food safety is important if you are eating gluten-free or not. Here are some important food safety tips that apply to all food preparation. You'll also find some additional tips to keep your gluten-free food separated from foods that contain gluten, thus keeping it safe for you to eat and enjoy.

Keep It Clean

Basic common-sense cleanliness is the best way to prevent the spread of bacteria and keep your food safe. Proper food handling is a must. Whether at the grocery store, taking food home, or fixing meals, keeping things clean ensures that your food not only tastes great but is safe to eat. Follow these rules:

1 Wash your hands. Always wash your hands in hot, soapy water before, during, and after cooking and eating. Wash them for at least 20 seconds. This is the best way to prevent

the spread of bacteria and viruses (and prevent cold and flu), and is the best way to keep you and your food safe.

2 Keep everything that touches food clean. Bacteria can hitch rides around your kitchen on dirty utensils, sponges, dishcloths, plates, knives, and cutting boards. Use fresh towels and dishcloths every day. And always clean your cutting board or work surface with hot soapy water after each use.

3 Do not cross-contaminate raw meat with raw vegetables. Keep raw meat, poultry, fish, and their juices from coming into contact with any other foods that will not be cooked. Use one cutting board for cutting raw meat and another one for cutting up vegetables and fruits.

Avoid cross-contamination from gluten to other items in your kitchen by keeping a separate cutting board to cut ingredients for gluten-free recipes. If possible, keep separate mixers and

mixing bowls, utensils, and measuring cups for gluten-free cooking as well.

Keep Cold Foods Cold and Hot Foods Hot

1 Keep your refrigerator and freezer cold. Keep your refrigerator between 35-40°F and your freezer at or below 0° F. Immediately put all meat and dairy items in the refrigerator or freezer after you buy them—never leave them in a warm car or trunk.

Use uncooked roasts, steaks, and chops within 2 days if they are in the refrigerator. All chicken, turkey, ground meat, or fish should be cooked within 1 or 2 days. If you aren't going to eat it right away, freeze it. Most meats can be kept in the freezer for up to 6 months. To thaw meat, place it in the fridge on a plate or in a bag. Never just leave it on the counter to thaw. After the meat is thawed, cook it right away—within a day. Never refreeze raw meat.

2 Refrigerate cooked foods promptly after serving (within 2 hours of cooking). Store leftovers in small containers rather than large ones so they chill quickly in the fridge. Never let foods sit out after cooking because bacteria can quickly grow.

3 When reheating foods, heat thoroughly. Leftovers should be well-heated or boiled before being served again. Reheat only the amount needed for the meal. Do not reheat the entire amount unless all can be consumed at the meal. Do not reheat leftovers more than once.

4 Most meat and poultry foods should be cooked until there is no red or pink color in the meat. That includes all ground meats like ground beef, ground turkey, and sausage. Beef roasts and steaks can be served with a slight pink color left in the middle if

you like it that way. But the meat has to reach a certain temperature before the bacteria are killed, so don't take risks. Use a meat thermometer to be sure meats are thoroughly cooked. Rotate or stir meat frequently during cooking to ensure all sides and the interior are evenly cooked, especially in the microwave, which can cook foods unevenly.

Be Sure it is Safe

1 When preparing canned vegetables and soups, always bring them to a full boil. If using home-canned vegetables, boil for at least 20 minutes. This will kill most bacteria, some of which can be deadly. If the top of the lid is not flat on the glass canning jar or there is a bulge on a purchased metal can, that means it is spoiled—throw it out before tasting it!

2 Never partially cook foods and then set them aside to finish cooking later. Cook your food completely at one time; dividing the cooking time may allow bacteria to grow.

3 Never eat under cooked eggs. Make sure both the egg white and yolk are firm and opaque, not runny and translucent. Avoid eating cookie dough or cake batter that contains raw eggs.

4 Read the labels. Don't buy anything if the "sell by" date has expired. Follow the "use by" or "freeze by" dates on a package. Most dairy products are good for one week after the "sell by" date. After that, throw them out.

USDA Recommended Safe Minimum Internal Temperatures	
• Steaks and Roasts	145°F
• Ground Beef	160°F
• Pork	160°F
• Egg Dishes	160°F
• Chicken Breasts	165°F
• Whole Poultry	165°F
• Fish	145°F

BETTER IF USED BY
02JUL2011 CI035716 C

RESEALABLE BAG INSIDE
BEST BEFORE:
17JUN2011
06:46

About Nutrition

Nutrition is important for everyone, but individuals on a gluten-free diet must be especially careful to consume enough of certain vitamins and minerals.

The U.S. food supply is enriched and fortified with certain nutrients to prevent vitamin deficiencies, but unfortunately for people on a gluten-free diet, most of the enrichment is accomplished via wheat flour. In the U.S., the law dictates that wheat flour is enriched with folic acid, iron, and B vitamins (B1 (thiamin), B2 (riboflavin), and B3 (niacin). Enrichment with calcium and vitamin D are optional. Therefore, people on a gluten-free diet must be aware of their intakes of these essential nutrients. Deficiency in any of these nutrients can cause serious results.

The only commonly enriched gluten-free product is white rice, but it is important to note that the nutrients will wash away if you rinse the rice before cooking.

Iron, B vitamins, and vitamin D are all essential nutrients for which individuals on a gluten-free diet must pay extra attention. B vitamins, including thiamin, riboflavin, niacin, and folic acid, serve many functions in the body, including vital roles in metabolism and energy production. In addition, they are required for red blood cell production and function and DNA synthesis and repair. B vitamins are water-soluble vitamins, meaning that the body cannot store them so they must be consumed every day.

B vitamins are found in many foods including meats, fish, vegetables, and grains. However, because whole grains and enriched flours are especially high in vitamin B, individuals on a gluten-free diet are more likely to have a deficiency in one or all of the B vitamins. If there is a deficiency, every B vitamin leads to certain symptoms. Deficiency of thiamin (B1), called beriberi, leads to nervous system problems including weight loss, irregular heartbeat, and impaired sensory perceptions. Deficiency of riboflavin (B2), causes symptoms including inflammation of the tongue, high sensitivity to sunlight, and cracks in the lips. Deficiency of niacin (B3), called pellagra, leads to nervous systems problems including dementia, weakness, and insomnia. Deficiency of folic acid causes symptoms such as fatigue and weakness. Because B vitamin deficiencies are more likely among people on a gluten-free diet, it may be a good idea to discuss taking a B complex vitamin with a doctor or dietitian.

Iron deficiency is often considered to be the most common essential nutrient deficiency in the world. Iron is an essential mineral required for oxygen transport, cell growth and differentiation, enzyme funtion, and many other important functions. Two types of iron are found in food: heme iron and nonheme iron. Heme iron, derived from hemoglobin, is only found in animal products. Nonheme iron is found in plant products. The best sources of iron are animal products such as beef, liver, oysters, clams, turkey, and chicken. Fortified cereals are also good sources of iron, as are many legumes. Iron deficiency is common in untreated celiacs (those eating gluten in their diet). When the small intestine is damaged from celiac disease, iron cannot be efficiently absorbed and the person may develop iron deficiency. A person with iron deficiency will display symptoms such as fatigue, decreased immunity, anemia, hair loss, and weakness.

It is important to note that because the body can store excess iron, iron toxicity is a serious risk. Therefore, if taking an iron supplement, be careful not to take more than the recommended dose of iron each day. Always keep pills away from children. Overdosing on iron supplements can quickly lead to death.

In recent years, scientists have discovered more and more important functions of vitamin D. Known as the "sunshine vitamin", vitamin D is actually a hormone synthesized in our skin by UV light and cholesterol. In theory, our bodies should be able to produce enough vitamin D from sunlight to meet our needs. However, a person's ability to produce vitamin D varies greatly by season, latitude, race, amount of sun exposure and clothing, amount of skin pigmentation, and age. The most vitamin D production is possible in summer, at lower latitudes

(nearer to the equator), for younger people with whiter or less pigmented skin. Vitamin D serves many functions in the human body, including controlling calcium and phosphorous levels in the blood.

Adequate amounts of vitamin D are required for healthy bones and teeth, normal thyroid function, and immune system function. In addition, vitamin D helps control cell growth in several body tissues. Vitamin D is naturally found in only a handful of foods. The richest sources are fish liver oils, herring, salmon, sardines, liver, shrimp, and egg yolks. However, vitamin D is now fortified in many foods, including milk, soymilk, butter, dried milk, and several breakfast cereals.

Vitamin D deficiency may lead to decreased muscle function, thyroid problems, falls, osteoporosis, and fractures. Several research studies indicate that proper vitamin D supplementation can decrease the risk of these problems. Studies show that vitamin D and calcium supplements improve bone density and strength, prevent fractures, reverse thyroid problems, improve muscle function, and help heal skin lesions.

Fiber is also a serious concern for individuals on a gluten-free diet. Gluten-free foods tend to use more starches and refined grains instead of whole grains. Try to incorporate at least three servings of whole grains into your diet each day to increase intake of fiber, vitamins, and minerals.

Of course, before making any dietary changes, talk to your doctor or dietitian. Every person has specific needs that can only be evaluated by a medical professional.

Whole grain gluten-free foods include:

- Corn/corn meal/flour
- Corn tortillas/chips
- Popcorn
- Buckwheat flour
- Brown rice/brown rice flour
- Sorghum/sorghum flour
- Wild rice
- Amaranth/amaranth flour
- Quinoa/quinoa flour
- Teff/teff flour
- Millet/millet flour

Glossary of Cooking Terms

Al dente: Italian for "to the tooth." It describes pasta that is cooked until it offers a slight resistance when bitten into, rather than cooked until soft. When cooking gluten-free pasta this stage may be more difficult to accomplish.

Bake: To cook food, covered or uncovered, using the direct, dry heat of an oven. The term is usually used to describe the cooking of cakes, desserts, casseroles, and breads.

Baste: To brush or spoon food as it cooks with melted fat or the cooking juices from the dish. Basting prevents foods from drying out and adds color and flavor.

Batter: An uncooked, wet mixture that can be spooned or poured, as with cakes, pancakes, and muffins. Batters usually contain some type of flour, eggs, and milk as their base. Some thin batters are used to coat foods before deep frying such as in a tempura batter.

Beat: To make a mixture smooth by briskly stirring it with a spoon, fork, wire whisk, rotary beater, or electric mixer.

Bias-slice: To slice a food crosswise at a 45-degree angle.

Blanch: To cook raw ingredients such as vegetables briefly in boiling water—generally for about 1 minute—and then plunge immediately and briefly into an ice water bath to stop the cooking process and preserve color and nutrients.

Blend: To combine two or more ingredients together with a spoon, beater, or blender.

Boil: To heat a liquid to its boiling point, until bubbles break the surface. "Boil" also means to cook food in a boiling liquid.

Bone: To remove the bones from meat, fish, or poultry. Use a sharp boning knife and angle the blade toward the bone to avoid tearing or nicking the flesh.

Braise: To cook food, tightly covered, in a small amount of liquid at low heat for a long period of time. Sometimes the food is first browned in fat. The long, slow cooking tenderizes meats by gently breaking down their fibers.

Broil: To cook food below direct, dry heat. When broiling, position the broiler pan and its rack so that the surface of the food (not the rack) is the specified distance from the heat source.

Broth: The strained clear liquid in which meat, poultry, or fish has simmered with vegetables and herbs. It is similar to stock and can be used interchangeably with it. Reconstituted bouillon can also be used when broth is specified.

Brown: To cook a food in a skillet, broiler, or oven to add flavor and aroma and develop a rich, desirable color on the outside and moistness on the inside.

Brush: To apply a liquid, like a glaze, to the surface of food using a pastry brush.

Butterfly: To split food (meat, fish, poultry) down the center, cutting almost, but not completely through. The two halves are then opened flat to resemble a butterfly.

Caramelize: To heat sugar until it liquefies and become a clear caramel syrup ranging in color from golden to dark brown. Fruits and vegetables with natural sugars can be caramelized by sautéing, roasting, or grilling—giving them a sweet flavor and golden glaze.

Carve: To cut or slice cooked meat, poultry, fish, or game into serving-size pieces.

Chiffonade: To slice into very thin strips or shreds. Literally translated from French, the term means "made of rags". Often used on fresh herbs or lettuce.

Chill: To cool food to below room temperature over ice or in the refrigerator. When recipes call for chilling foods, it should be done in the refrigerator not the freezer.

Chop: To cut food into irregular bite-size pieces using a knife. A food processor may also be used to chop food. Chopped food is more coarsely cut than minced food.

Cream: To beat a fat, such as butter or shortening either alone or with sugar, to a light, fluffy consistency. This may be done by hand with a wooden spoon or with an electric mixer. This process incorporates air into the fat so baked products have a lighter texture and a better volume. This is a good way to add "lift" when making gluten-free breads, cookies, and cakes.

Crimp: To pinch or press pastry or dough together using your fingers, a fork, or another utensil. Mostly done for a pie crust edge.

Crisp-tender: A term that describes the state of vegetables that have been cooked until just tender but still somewhat crunchy. At this stage, a fork can be inserted with a little pressure.

Curdle: To cause coagulated pieces of protein to develop. This can occur when dairy foods such as milk or sour cream are heated to too high a temperature or combined with an acidic food, such as lemon juice.

Cure: To treat food by one of several methods for preservation purposes. Examples are smoking, pickling in an acid, corning with acid and salt, and salt curing, which removes water. Some cured meats also contain gluten which is added in the curing process.

Cut-in: To work a solid fat, such as shortening, butter, or margarine, into dry ingredients. This is usually done with a pastry blender, two knives in a crisscross fashion, fingertips, or a food processor.

Dash: Refers to a small amount of seasoning that is added to food. It is generally between $\frac{1}{16}$ and $\frac{1}{8}$ teaspoon. The term is often used for liquid ingredients, such as bottled hot pepper sauce.

Deep-fry: To cook food in hot fat or oil deep enough so that the food is completely or nearly covered. The temperature of the fat is extremely important. Fat at the correct temperature will produce food with a crisp, dry exterior and moist interior. An average fat temperature for deep-frying is 375°F, but the temperature varies according

to the food being fried. Use a deep fryer, an electric fry pan, or a heavy pot and a good kitchen thermometer for deep-frying.

Devein: To remove the blackish-gray vein from the back of shrimp. The vein can be removed with a special utensil called a deveiner or with the tip of a sharp knife. Small and medium shrimp need deveining for aesthetic purposes only. However, because the veins in large shrimp contain grit, they should always be removed.

Dice: To cut food into small cubes (about $\frac{1}{8}$- to $\frac{1}{4}$-inch).

Double boiler: A two-pan arrangement where one pan nests partway inside the other. The lower pot holds simmering water that gently cooks heat-sensitive food in the upper pot.

Drain: To pour off fat or liquid from food, often using a colander.

Dredge: To lightly coat food that is going to be fried with some type of flour, bread crumbs, or cornmeal. The coating helps to brown the food and provides a crunchy surface. Heavier gluten-free flours work best for dredging.

Drizzle: To randomly pour a liquid, such as powdered sugar icing, in a thin stream over food.

Fillet: (verb) To create a fillet of fish or meat by cutting away the bones. Fish and boning knives help produce clean fillets. (noun) A piece of meat or fish that has no bones.

Flake: To gently break food into small, flat pieces—usually done with a fork.

Flour: (verb) To coat or dust a food or utensil with a type of flour—with or without gluten. Food may be floured before cooking to add texture and improve browning. (noun) A substance that has been ground usually from a grain or legume such as wheat flour, rice flour, quinoa flour, bean flour, etc.

Flute: To make a decorative impression in food, usually a pie crust or tart.

Fold: To combine a light mixture like beaten egg whites with a much heavier mixture such as cake batter. In a large bowl, place the lighter mixture on top of the heavier one. Starting at the back of the bowl, using the edge of a rubber spatula, cut down through the middle of both mixtures, across the bottom of the bowl and up the near side. Rotate the bowl a quarter turn and repeat. This process gently combines the two mixtures.

Fry: To cook food (non-submerged) in hot fat or oil over moderate to high heat.

Grate: To reduce a large piece of food to coarse or fine threads by rubbing it against a rough, serrated surface, usually on a grater. A food processor, fitted with the appropriate blades, can also be used for grating. The food that is being grated should be firm. Food that needs to be grated can be refrigerated first for easier grating.

Grease: To coat a utensil, such as a baking pan or skillet, with a thin layer of fat or oil. A pastry brush works well to grease pans. Also refers to fat released from meat and poultry during cooking.

Grill: (verb) To cook food on a grill over hot coals or other heat source. The intense heat creates a crust on the surface of the food which seals in the juices. The grill should be clean and must be heated before the food is laid on it.

Grind: To reduce food to small pieces by running it through a grinder. Food can be ground to different degrees, from fine to coarse.

Julienne: To cut food into thin sticks. Food is cut with a sharp knife into even slices, then into strips.

Knead: To mix and work dough into a smooth, elastic mass if using flour with gluten. By hand, kneading is done with a pressing-folding-turning action. In gluten-flour recipes, kneading is used to develop gluten, so gluten-free foods rarely use kneading.

Marble: To gently swirl one food into another. Marbling is usually done with light and dark batters for cakes or cookies.

Marinate: To soak food in a seasoned liquid mixture for a certain length of time. The purpose of marinating is to add flavor and/or tenderize the food.

Mash: To crush a food into a smooth and evenly textured state.

Mince: To cut food into very tiny pieces. Minced food is cut into smaller, finer pieces than diced food.

Mix: To stir or beat two or more foods together until they are thoroughly combined. May be done with an electric mixer, a rotary beater, or by hand with a wooden spoon.

Moisten: To add enough liquid to a dry ingredient or mixture to make it damp but not runny.

Open-faced: A sandwich prepared with just one piece of bread which is topped with a wide variety of meats, vegetables, or cheeses and heated or served cold.

Pan-broil: To cook a food, usually meat, in a skillet without added fat, removing any fat as it accumulates.

Parboil: To boil food briefly in water, cooking it only partially.

Pare: To remove the thin outer layer of foods using a paring knife or a vegetable peeler.

Peel: To remove the rind or skin from a fruit or vegetable using a knife or vegetable peeler.

Pinch: A small amount of a dry ingredient (the amount that can be pinched between a finger and the thumb).

Poach: To cook food by gently simmering in liquid at or just below the boiling point. The amount of the liquid and poaching temperature depends on the food being poached.

Preheat: To heat an oven or a utensil to a specific temperature before using it.

Process: To preserve food at home by canning, or to prepare food in a food processor.

Purée: To grind or mash food until completely smooth. This can be done using a food processor or blender or by pressing the food through a sieve.

Reconstitute: To bring a concentrated or condensed food, such as frozen fruit juice, to its original strength by adding water.

Reduce: To decrease the volume of a liquid by boiling it rapidly to cause evaporation.

Rice: (verb) To push cooked food such as potatoes through a perforated kitchen tool called a ricer. The resulting food looks like rice.

Roast: To oven-cook food in an uncovered pan. The food is exposed to high heat which produces a well-browned surface and seals in the juices. Reasonably tender pieces of meat or poultry should be used for roasting. Food that is going to be roasted for a long time should be covered to prevent drying out.

Sauté: To cook food quickly in a small amount of fat or oil, until brown, in a skillet or saute pan over direct heat. The sauté pan and fat must be hot before the food is added or the food will absorb oil and become soggy.

Sear: To brown meat, poultry, or fish quickly over very high heat either in a fry pan, under a broiler, or in a hot oven. Searing seals in the food's juices and provides a crisp tasty exterior. Seared food can then be eaten rare or roasted or braised to the desired degree of doneness.

Season: To add flavor to foods. Also to coat the cooking surface of a new pot or pan with vegetable oil then heat in a 350°F oven for about an hour. This smooths out the surface of new pots and pans, particularly cast-iron, and prevents foods from sticking.

Seed: (verb) To remove the seeds from fruits and vegetables.

Shred: To cut food into thin strips. This can be done by hand or by using a grater or food processor. Cooked meat can be shredded by pulling it apart with two forks.

Shuck: To remove the shells from seafood, such as oysters and clams, or the husks from corn.

Sieve: To strain liquids or particles of food through a sieve or strainer. Press the solids, using a ladle or wooden spoon, into the strainer to remove as much liquid and flavor as possible.

Sift: To pass dry ingredients through a fine mesh sifter so large pieces can be removed. The process also incorporates air to make some ingredients, such as flours, lighter.

Simmer: To cook food in liquid over gentle heat (just below the boiling point) low enough so that tiny bubbles just begin to break the surface.

Skewer: To spear small pieces of food on long, thin, pointed rods called skewers.

Skim: To remove any substance that accumulates on the top of a liquid, such as on a homemade broth or stock.

Skin: To remove the skin from food before or after cooking. Poultry, fish, and game are often skinned for reasons of appearance, taste, and diet.

Slice: (noun) A flat, usually thin, piece of food cut from a larger piece. (verb) The process of cutting flat, thin pieces.

Snip: To cut food, often fresh herbs or dried fruit, with kitchen shears or scissors into very small, uniform pieces using short, quick strokes.

Springform Pan: A round pan with high sides and a removable bottom usually used for cheesecakes and other types of cakes that are difficult to remove from a traditional pan. The bottom is removed by releasing a spring that holds the sides tight around it. This makes it easy to remove food from the pan.

Steam: To cook by using steam from boiling water in a covered pan. Steaming retains flavor, shape, texture, and nutrients better than boiling or poaching.

Steep: To allow a food, such as tea, to stand in water that is just below the boiling point in order to extract flavor or color.

Stew: (verb) To cook food in liquid for a long time until tender, usually in a covered pot. (noun) A recipe or mixture prepared this way.

Stir: To mix ingredients with a spoon or other utensil to combine them.

Stir-fry: A method of quickly cooking small pieces of food in a small amount of hot oil in a wok or skillet over medium-high heat while stirring constantly.

Stock: The strained clear liquid in which meat, poultry, or fish has been simmered with vegetables or herbs. It is similar to broth but is richer and more concentrated. Stock and broth can be used interchangeably; reconstituted bouillon can also be substituted for stock.

Tenderize: To make meat more tender by pounding with a mallet or marinating for varying periods of time.

Toast: (verb) The process of browning, crisping, or drying a food by exposing it to heat. Toasting coconut, nuts, and seeds helps develop their flavor. (noun) Bread after it has been exposed to heat.

Toss: To mix ingredients lightly by lifting and dropping them using two utensils.

Unleavened: The word which describes any baked good that has no leavening, such as yeast, baking powder, or baking soda.

Weeping: The appearance of liquid droplets as it separates out of a cooked food, such as jellies, custards, and meringues.

Whip: To beat ingredients such as egg whites or cream until light and fluffy. Air is incorporated into the ingredients as they are whipped, increasing their volume.

Whisk: To beat ingredients together until smooth, using a kitchen tool called a whisk.

Zest: To remove the outermost skin layers of citrus fruit using a knife, peeler or zester. When zesting, be careful not to remove the pith, the white layer between the zest and the flesh, which is bitter.

Resources

Celiac Organizations and Web Sites

American Celiac Disease Alliance
2504 Duxbury Place
Alexandria, VA 22308
(703) 622-3331
www.americanceliac.org

Celiac Disease Foundation
13251 Ventura Blvd
Studio City, CA 91604
(818) 990-2354
www.celiac.org

Celiac Sprue Association
P.O. Box 31700
Omaha, NE 68131-0700
(877) 272-4272
www.csaceliacs.org

Dining Card
Celiactravel.com
http://www.celiactravel.com/restaurant-cards.html

Gluten-Free Made Simple
www.gluten-freemadesimple.com
www.gfmadesimple.com

Gluten Intolerance Group
31214 124th Ave SE
Auburn, WA 98092
(253) 833-6655
www.gluten.net

Gluten-free All-Purpose Flour Mixes

Arrowhead Mills
4600 Sleepytime Dr
Boulder, CO 80301
(800) 434-4246
www.arrowheadmills.com

Bob's Red Mill Natural Foods
13521 SE Pheasant Court

Milwaukee, OR 97222
(800) 349-2173
www.bobsredmill.com

Domata Living Flour
P.O. Box 10
Fair Play, MO 65649
(417) 654-4010
www.domatalivingflour.com

Jules, LLC
7120 Minstrel Way, Ste 206
Columbia, MD 21045
(877) 236-3940
www.julesglutenfree.com

King Arthur Flour
135 US Route 5 South
Norwich, VT 05055
(800) 827-6836
www.kingarthurflour.com

Kinnikinnick Food
10940 120th Street
Edmonton, Alberta T5H 3P7, Canada
(877) 503-4466
www.kinnikinnick.com

Namaste Foods, LLC
P.O. Box 3133
Couer d'Alene, ID 83816
(866) 258-9493
www.namastefoods.com

Pamela's Products, Inc.
200 Clara Avenue
Ukiah, CA 95482
(707) 462-6605
www.pamelasproducts.com

Tom Sawyer
2155 West State Route 89A, Suite 106
Sedona, AZ 86336
(877) 372-8800
www.glutenfreeflour.com

Gluten-free Products

Chebe Bread Products
1840 Lundberg Drive
Spirit Lake, IA 51360
(800) 217-9510
www.chebe.com

ConAgra Foods, Inc
P.O. Box 3768
Omaha, NE 68103
(800) 858-6372 (Hunts)
(800) 726-4968 (Pam)
www.hunts.com
www.pam4you.com

Cookies Original BBQ Sauce
P.O. Box 458
Wall Lake, IA 51466
(800) 331-4995
www.cookiesbbq.com

Crisco & Dickinson's Lemon Curd
The J.M. Smucker Company
1 Strawberry Lane
Orrville, OH 44667
(800) 766-7309
www.crisco.com

Daisy Brand
12750 Merit Drive, Suite 600
Dallas, TX 75251
(877) 292-9830
www.daisybrand.com

Dei Fratelli (Pizza Sauce)
Hirzel Canning Co & Farms
Attn: Customer Service Department
411 Lemoyne Rd
Toledo, OH 43619
(877) 592-6736
www.deifratelli.com

French's – Reckitt Benckiser
North America
P.O. Box 224 Parsippany, NJ
07054
(800) 841-1256
www.frenchs.com

Frito-Lay
P.O. Box 660634
Dallas, TX 75266
(800) 352-4477
www.fritolay.com

General Mills, Inc
P.O. Box 9452
Minneapolis, MN 55440
(800) 248-7310
www.liveglutenfreely.com

Glutino
2055 Boul. Dagenais Quest
Laval, QC, H7L 5V1, Canada
(800) 363-3438
www.glutino.com

Heinz
(800) 255-5750
www.heinzketchup.com

Hellmann's/Best Foods Real
Mayonnaise
(800) 418-3275
www.hellmanns.us

Hodgson Mill
1100 Stevens Ave
Effingham, IL 62401
(800) 347-0105
www.hodgsonmill.com

Hormel Food Corporation
1 Hormel Place
Austin, MN 55912
(800) 523-4635
www.hormel.com

John Morrell
Consumer Affairs
P.O. Box 405020

Cincinnati, OH 45240
(800) 722-1127
www.johnmorrell.com

Johnsonville Sausage
P.O. Box 906
Sheboygan Falls, WI 53085
(888) 556-2728
www.johnsonville.com

Kraft Foods Global, Inc.
Global Consumer Relations
1 Kraft Court
Glenview, IL 60025
(877) 535-5666
www.kraftrecipes.com

La Choy
P.O. Box 57078
Irvine, CA 92619
(800) 252-0672
www.lachoy.com

Log Cabin Consumer Affairs
P.O. Box 3900
Peoria, IL 61612
www.logcabinsyrups.com

Mars, Inc. (Snickers)
www.snickers.com

McCormick & Company, Inc
18 Loveton Circle
Sparks, MD 21152
(800) 632-5847
www.mccormick.com

Nature's Path Foods
9100 Van Horne Way
Richmond, BC, Canada V6X 1W3
(888) 808-9505
www.naturespath.com

Nestle USA
Consumer Services Center
P.O. Box 2178
Wilkes-Barre, PA 18703
(800) 851-0512 (Baking Products)
(800) 854-8935 (Milk Products)

(800) 854-0374 (Pumpkin)
www.verybestbaking.com

Newman's Own
246 Post Road East
Westport, CT 06880
www.newmansown.com

Pace Foods
www.pacefoods.com

Quinoa Corporation
P.O. Box 279
Gardena, CA 90248
(310) 217-8125
www.quinoa.net

Skippy Peanut Butter
(866) 475-4779
www.peanutbutter.com

Superior Quality Foods (Better
Than Bouillon)
2355 E. Francis Street
Ontario, CA 91761
(800) 300-4210
www.superiortouch.com

Tabasco
whatscooking@tabasco.com
www.tabasco.com

Tinkyada Rice Pasta
120 Melford Drive, Unit 8
Scarborough, Ontario, Canada
M1B 2X5
(416) 609-00116
www.tinkyada.com

Udi's Gluten Free Foods
7010 Broadway Stuite #430
Denver, CO 80221
(303) 657-6366
www.udisglutenfree.com

V8 Juice
www.v8juice.com

Index

Index

Index